SPLAY ANTHEM

ALSO BY NATHANIEL MACKEY

Poetry Books and Chapbooks

Four for Trane
Septet for the End of Time
Outlantish
Song of the Andoumboulou: 18–20
Four for Glenn
Eroding Witness
School of Udhra
Whatsaid Serif
Nod House
Blue Fasa

Fiction

Bedouin Hornbook
Djbot Baghostus's Run
Atet A.D.
Bass Cathedral
From a Broken Bottle Traces of Perfume Still Emanate
Late Arcade

Criticism

*Discrepant Engagement: Dissonance, Cross-Culturality, and
    Experimental Writing*
Paracritical Hinge: Essays, Talks, Notes, Interviews

Anthologies

Moment's Notice: Jazz in Poetry and Prose (with Art Lange)

Recordings

Strick: Song of the Andoumboulou 16–25

SPLAY ANTHEM

NATHANIEL MACKEY

A NEW DIRECTIONS BOOK

Acknowledgments: Some of these poems first appeared in the following publications: *Bombay Gin, Boston Review, Boxkite, Callaloo, Conjunctions, Enough, Facture, First Intensity, Fourteen Hills: The SFSU Review, The Germ, Hambone, Hotel Amerika, Indiana Review, Journal of Caribbean Literatures, Jubilat, Kunapipi, Luna, Mandorla, New American Writing, No: A Journal of the Arts, Smartish Pace, Sulfur, Writing on Air, Xcp: Cross-Cultural Poetics.*

"Song of the Andoumboulou: 42," "Go Left Out of Shantiville," "Song of the Andoumboulou: 44," and "Glenn on Monk's Mountain" were published as a chapbook, *Four for Glenn*, by Chax Press in 2002.

Manufactured in the United States of America
New Directions Books are printed on acid-free paper.
First published as a New Directions Paperbook 1032 (NDP1032) in 2006

Library of Congress Cataloging-in-Publication Data
Mackey, Nathaniel, 1947–
Splay anthem / Nathaniel Mackey.
p. cm.
ISBN-13: 978-0-8112-1652-4 (alk. paper)
ISBN-10: 0-8112-1652-7 (alk. paper)
I. Title.
PS3563.A3166S65 2006
811'.53—dc22   2005035051

10 9 8 7 6 5

New Directions Books are published for James Laughlin
by New Directions Publishing Corporation
80 Eighth Avenue, New York, NY 10011

for Wilson

CONTENTS

PREFACE

Splay Anthem takes up and takes farther two ongoing serial poems, *Song of the Andoumboulou* and *"Mu,"* the two now understood as two and the same, each the other's understudy. Each is the other, each is both, announcedly so in this book by way of number, in earlier books not so announcedly so. By turns visibly and invisibly present, each is the other's twin or contagion, each entwines the other's crabbed advance. They have done so, unannouncedly, from the beginning, shadowed each other from the outset, having a number of things in common, most obviously music. Each was given its impetus by a piece of recorded music from which it takes its title, the Dogon "Song of the Andoumboulou" in one case, Don Cherry's *"Mu" First Part* and *"Mu" Second Part* in the other.

François Di Dio, in the liner notes to *Les Dogon,* his 1956 recording of Dogon music for Disques Ocora, says the song of the Andoumboulou is addressed to the spirits. Part of the Dogon funeral rites, it begins with sticks marking time on a drum's head, joined in short order by a lone, laconic voice – gravelly, raspy, reluctant – recounting the creation of the world and the advent of human life. Other voices, likewise reticent, dry, join in, eventually build into song, a scratchy, low-key chorus. From time to time a yodeling shriek breaks out in the background. Song subsided, another lone voice eulogizes the deceased, reciting his genealogy, bestowing praise, listing all the places where he set foot while alive, a spiral around the surrounding countryside. Antelope-horn trumpets blast and bleat when the listing ends, marking the entry of the deceased into the other life, evoking, Di Dio writes, "the wail of a new-born child, born into a terrifying world."

Multi-instrumentalist Don Cherry, best known as a trumpeter, includes voice among the instruments used on the *"Mu"* albums and resorts to a sort of dove-coo baby talk on one piece, "Teo-Teo-Can," emitting sounds that might accompany the tickling of a baby's chin if not made by the baby itself. It recalls Amiri Baraka's comment on hearing a John Coltrane solo that consisted of playing the head of "Confirmation" again and again, twenty times or so: "like watching a grown man learning to speak." In both cases, as with the Dogon trumpet burst and as it's put in "Song of the Andoumboulou: 58," one is "back / at / some beginning," some extremity taking one back to animating constraint. The antelope-horn trumpet's blast and bleat, Cherry's ludic warble and Trane's recursive quandary are variations on music as gnostic announcement, ancient rhyme, that of end and beginning, gnostic accent or note that cuts both ways.

But not only music. "Mu" (in quotes to underscore its whatsaidness) is also lingual and imaginal effect and affect, myth and mouth in the Greek form *muthos* that Jane Harrison, as Charles Olson was fond of noting, calls "a re-utterance or pre-utterance, ... a focus of emotion," surmising the first muthos to have been "simply the interjectional utterance *mu*." "Mu" is also lingual and erotic allure, mouth and muse, mouth not only noun but verb and muse likewise, lingual and imaginal process, prod and process. It promises verbal and romantic enhancement, graduation to an altered state, momentary thrall translated into myth. Proffered from time immemorial, poetry's perennial boon, it thrives on quixotic persistence, the increment or enablement language affords, promise and impossibility rolled into one (Anuncia/Nunca). "Mu" carries a theme of utopic reverie, a theme of lost ground and elegiac allure recalling the Atlantis-like continent Mu, thought by some during the late nineteenth century and early twentieth century to have existed long ago in the Pacific. The places named in the song of the Andoumboulou, set foot on by the deceased while alive but lost or taken away by death, could be called "Mu." Any longingly imagined, mourned or remembered place, time, state, or condition can be called "Mu."

Wandering and run come into both series, shaded or shadowed by rut, the condition they seek to undo or to come to new terms with, as though roust, rout, rouse and the like were rut itself differently understood, an itineracy endemic to the medium echoing the flight and fugitivity the poems point to and report. The poems' we, a lost tribe of sorts, a band of nervous travelers, know nothing if not locality's discontent, ground gone under. Sonic semblance's age-old promise, rhyme's reason, the consolation they seek in song, accents and further aggravates movement. The songs are increasingly songs of transit. Sameness and similitude, dispersed, worry location, fret constituting historical shorthand. Glamorizations by the tourist industry notwithstanding, travel and migration for the vast majority of people have been and continue to be unhappy if not catastrophic occurrences brought about by unhappy if not catastrophic events: the Middle Passage, the Spanish Expulsion, the Irish Potato Famine, conscripted military service, indentured labor systems, pursuit of asylum....

I wasn't aware of the Andoumboulou's relevance to ground gone under until I read Marcel Griaule and Germaine Dieterlen's *The Pale Fox* in the late 1980s, though the whispered, sotto voce recitation and singing heard on the "Song of the Andoumboulou" track on *Les Do-*

gon planted an intuitive theme of underness when I first heard it in the early 1970s. From Griaule and Dieterlen I learned that the Andoumboulou are a failed, earlier form of human being in Dogon cosmogony, one of the results of the pale fox Ogo's cosmic revolt and incestuous penetration of the earth in pursuit of his lost female twin. The Andoumboulou, along with the Yeban who were born of that union and in turn gave birth to them, live underground, inhabiting holes in the earth.

Given the centrality of various forms of graphic inscription in Dogon cosmology, the cosmogonic potency and role of sign, figure, drawing, trace, diagram, outline, image, mark, design and so on (for all of which the Dogon use a careful, hairsplitting terminology), along with the strikingly tactile, abraded vocality, the grating, "graphic" tone and timbre of the song of the Andoumboulou itself, I couldn't help thinking of the Andoumboulou as not simply a failed, or flawed, earlier form of human being but a rough draft of human being, the work-in-progress we continue to be. The commonplace expression "man's inhumanity to man" has long acknowledged our andoumboulouousness. The song of the Andoumboulou is one of striving, strain, abrasion, an all but asthmatic song of aspiration. Lost ground, lost twinness, lost union and other losses variably inflect that aspiration, a wish, among others, to be we, that of the recurring two, the archetypal lovers who visit and revisit the poems, that of some larger collectivity an anthem would celebrate.

The song of the Andoumboulou is Dogon deep song, Dogon *cante jondo*. As in *cante jondo*, inauspicious prospects attenuate the voice. Rasp and aridity hold sway, affliction and response to affliction – "rasp our lone / resort," as I put it in *Whatsaid Serif.* As in *cante jondo*, attenuation extends the voice; it stretches it, strings it out. A subjection to qualm and qualification is the semantic equivalent of such attenuation, "rub's accretion" as it's called in "Sound and Cerement," strain and abrasion played out as predication. Rub a kind of erasure, statement backtracks or breaks off, ellipses abound, assertion and retraction volley, assertion and supplementation: addition, subtraction, revision, conundrum, nuance, amendment, tweak. This too is a kind of movement, a kind of mobility, an aspect of ground gone under, loss or lack of assurance.

Serial form lends itself to andoumboulouous liminality, the draft unassured extension knows itself to be. Provisional, ongoing, the serial poem moves forward and backward both, repeatedly "back / at / some beginning," repeatedly circling or cycling back, doing so with such adamance as to call forward and back into question and suggest an eccentric step to the side – as though, driven to distraction by shortcircuiting options, it can only be itself beside itself. So it is that *"Mu"* is also *Song of the Andoumboulou, Song of the Andoumboulou* also *"Mu."* H.D.'s crazed geese, circling above the spot that was once Atlantis or the Hesperides or the Islands of the Blest, come to mind, as do John Coltrane's wheeling, spiraling runs as if around or in pursuit of some lost or last note, lost or last amenity: a tangential, verging movement out (outlantish). The ring shout comes to mind, as do the rings of Saturn, the planet adopted by Sun Ra, one of whose albums, *Atlantis,* opens with a piece called "Mu."

Emblematic of an outside seriality wishes to reach, ringing is sonic resurfacing, a step up as well as out. It invites echo, reverberation, overtone, undertone, resonance and repetition. In seriality, rasp is recursive form, a net of echoes; it catches. One hears this in the music of Glenn Spearman, a San Francisco Bay Area tenor saxophonist to whom four of the poems herein, published in 2002 as a chapbook entitled *Four for Glenn,* are dedicated, poems in which *rung* is both noun and verb, in which *climb,* we're reminded, rhymes with *chime.* The chapbook title deliberately echoes that of my first chapbook, *Four for Trane,* itself taken from and echoing that of Archie Shepp's 1965 album dedicated to John Coltrane. Appropriately so, as Spearman, who died in 1998 at age 51, was a saxophonist in the Coltrane tradition, a tradition worked and ramified by such musicians as Shepp, Albert Ayler (whose music was likened to a Salvation Army band on LSD, as relevant a gloss on splay anthem as any), Pharoah Sanders and, of particular importance to Spearman, Frank Wright, with whom he studied and worked in Paris in the 1970s. Appropriately so in other ways as well, as Glenn's music could be pointedly echoic. Toward the end of his 1993 composition "Thinking of Frank," he quotes from the piece Wright wrote in memory of Trane, "One for John." Here echo is homage, lineage, "a school of ancestors" as Wilson Harris would say. Echo is also the specter of dispersed identity and community, staggered adjunction or address recalling Robert Duncan's "commune of poetry."

One echoes oneself as well, a consequence of time not to be avoided that seriality makes conscious work of, "Song of the Andoumboulou: 48" harking back to "Song of the Andoumboulou: 10," three titles in the *"Mu"* series recalling my essay "Sound and Sentiment, Sound and Symbol" and so on. One finds oneself circling, the susceptibility of previous moments in the work to revisitation and variation conducing to a theme of articulation's non-ultimacy, a theme too of mortality and new life. Earlier moments can be said to die and live on as echo and rearticulation, riff and recontextualization, alteration and reconception. The song of the Andoumboulou is one of burial and rebirth, *mu* momentary utterance extended into ongoing myth, an impulse toward signature, self-elaboration, finding and losing itself. The word for this is *ythm* (clipped rhythm, anagrammatic myth). Revisitation suggests that what was and, by extension, what is might be otherwise. "By myth," Olson quotes Harrison quoting Aristotle, "I mean the arrangement of the incidents" – this in advancing a sense of alternative, "a special view of history."

Against presumptions of an objective ordering of history Olson elsewhere poses "what we know went on, the dream." This applies to present as well as past history, which is why we know or think we know it. Dream, the tendency of events to overwhelm rendition, is also rendition's wish to compete, often in the form of telic assurances, positing eventual if not immanent transparency and redemption. Even the gnostic indictment of history as nightmare and delusion carries a prescribed awakening which, if gnosis is to be gnostic enough, would have to allow it might itself be only a dream. When rendition knows or thinks it knows this, dream and awakening relativize each other. As Ed Roberson puts it, "to dream is not to dream / if waking up is never finished." When rendition knows or thinks it knows this, awakening to rather than from the dream is as close as one gets and, even in subscribing to a salvific history, any march events can be said to comprise can only be crablike, splay.

As much the condition the poem aspires to as music, dream can be so much and mean so much one wonders what waking up offers. The inhabitants of Atlantis are said to have been dreamless, which presumably means they were happy, without discontent, but the Aranda of Australia, the subject of Géza Róheim's *The Eternal Ones of the Dream*, a book important to Duncan's *H.D. Book*, actively seek to remain in the dream, to be in more than one place at a time. Dreamtime, *altjeringa*, is a way of enduring reality, the fact that dream itself borders on dread notwithstanding, the fact that as nightmare, more than bordering, it crosses over notwithstanding. It is also a way of challenging reality, a sense in which to dream is not to dream but to replace waking with realization, an ongoing process of testing or contesting reality, subjecting it to change or a demand for change.

Dream too is a school of ancestors, one of the altered states in which the dead reappear, one of such states the we in these pages pursue. (The Aranda word for dream also means ancestor.) Among the Dogon, elders get drunk on millet beer, into which the souls of the disgruntled dead have crept. These are the dead who have not yet been properly laid to rest by their surviving kin, those for whom the required rites have not yet been performed, the required altars not yet built, the attendant libations not yet poured. They get into the beer, under whose influence the elders accost the community with insults and accusations, openly muttering abuse along the streets, in the marketplace and elsewhere. "The dead are dying of thirst," they say, a reminder intended to make its way to the kin in question. This pronouncement has echoed and been revisited and varied in poems going back to "Song of the Andoumboulou: 1," an echo that continues in *Splay Anthem*, suggesting not only debts to history or the dead or the past, a neglect of history or the dead or the past, but other non-observances only an alteration of mind might set right. Could "The dead are dying of thirst" apply to the living dead wanting to awake, wanting more life, wanting more from life? An appetite for acknowledgment and the change it can bring drives andoumboulouous we.

This thirst or demand or desire sounds a sometimes dark note, a note whose not yet fulfilled promise bends it, turns it blue. A desperate accent or inflection runs through seriality's recourse to repetition, an apprehension of limits we find ourselves up against again and again, limits we'd get beyond if we could. This qualifies the promise of advance and possibility the form otherwise proffers, the feeling for search it's conducive to complicated by senses of constraint. Circularity, a figure for wholeness, also connotes boundedness. Recursiveness can mark a sense of deprivation fostered by failed advance, a sense of alarm and insufficiency pacing a dark, even desperate measure, but this dark accent or inflection issues from a large appetite or even a utopic appetite or, better – invoking Duke Ellington's neologism – a blutopic appetite. Seriality's mix of utopic ongoingness and recursive constraint is blutopic, an idealism shaped or shaded by blue, in-between foreboding, blue, dystopic apprehension of the way the world is.

Recursiveness, incantatory insistence, is liturgy and libation, repeated ritual sip, a form of sonic observance aiming to undo the obstruction it reports. It plies memory, compensatory possession, reminiscent regard and regret. "The dead are dying of thirst" I first read around the time I read a line of Edward Dahlberg's that I tend to hear it in conversation with: "Memory is our day of water tutored by want." I hear it in conversation with Robert Creeley's reading of Dahlberg's aperçu as well. "It means," Creeley writes, "that we remember what we have, because we do not have it." Recursion is conjunctive deprivation and possession, phantom limb, as if certain aroused and retained relations among consonants and vowels and progressions of accent were compensatory arms we reach with, compensatory legs we cross over on.

Thus the chronically resided in, repeatedly arrived at Nub (nubbed version Nuh), place name and diagnosis fraught with senses of diminishment: failed extension or falling short but not only that, the proverbial nub drawn back from overreaching but not only that, phantom limb's compensated occasion but not only that, remnant wish but not only that. I don't know everything Nub is or implies or might mean (nubbed version of Numb as well as Nubia but not only that), only that it offered itself, the predicament it appeared intent on naming having to do with the dreariness of recent events as well as ontology, the imperial, flailing republic of Nub the United States has become, the shrunken place the earth has become, planet Nub. In a match that seems to have been made in hell, hijacked airliners echo and further entrench a hijacked election, cycles of recriminatory assault further confirming a regime of echo the poem's recourse to echo would cure homeopathically if it could. The long odds against that are enough to induce an exasperated scat or an incipient stutter or a lapse into baby talk (Nuh), an impulse "to caricature history" and "to become Idiot Nameless" as Harris puts it, the advent of "unsay's / day" as it is in "Song of the Andoumboulou: 58."

Such odds are enough to induce bird talk and to condition bird talk, talk by birds and for the birds, the prototype for music and poetic language among the Kaluli of Papua New Guinea, as well as for Olson, who, addressing poets, says that "the Airs which belong to Birds have / led our lives to be these things instead of Kings." Steven Feld writes about the Kaluli in *Sound and Sentiment*, a book which, along with Victor Zuckerkandl's *Sound and Symbol*, gives the essay "Sound and Sentiment, Sound and Symbol" its title and is recalled by three titles in the *"Mu"* series: "Sound and Semblance," "Sound and Sentience," "Sound and Cerement." Feld relates a story the Kaluli tell regarding the origin of poetry and music, the myth of the boy who became a *muni* bird, a kind of fruitdove with a bright purple red beak. The boy turns into a *muni* bird and resorts to its cry when his older sister denies him food, a semi-sung, semi-wept complaint the Kaluli identify as the origin and essence of music and poetic language. To poetize or sing is to talk like a bird, a way with words and sound given rise to by a break in social relations, a denial of kinship and social sustenance, as if the break were a whistling fissure, an opening blown on like a flute. "Mu," then, also as in *muni*.

A sign of estrangement, to poetize or sing is to risk irrelevance, to be haunted by poetry's or music's possible irrelevance ("Tell it to the birds"), but nothing could be more relevant than estrangement, involved as we are in what Harris calls "the funeral of an age," an age of global intimacy and predation. *Gisalo,* the most Kaluli of Kaluli song forms and the one that most closely approximates the sound of the *muni* bird, has the melodic contour of the *muni* bird's cry and is a form of singing that crosses over into weeping. Like the song of the Andoumboulou, it is addressed to the spirits. The Kaluli sing it at funerals and they sing it during spirit-medium seances as well. Kaluli poetics posits poetry and music as quintessentially elegiac but also restorative, not only lamenting violated connection but aiming to reestablish connection, as if the entropy that gives rise to them is never to be given the last word. As with the Dogon trumpet blast or the post-burial parade in New Orleans music, something undaunted wants to move no matter how inauspicious the prospects, advance no matter how pained or ungainly.

... a place of encounter and connivance ...
—Édouard Glissant, *Poetics of Relation*

and all motion
is a crab
—Charles Olson, "The Moon Is the Number 18"

I

BRAID

because to dream is not to dream
if waking up is never finished

—Ed Roberson, "dreaming has made
more strict the terms of dream-
ing"

ANDOUMBOULOUOUS BRUSH

—"mu" fifteenth part—

He turned his head,
spoke to my clavicle,
whispered more than
spoke. Sprung bone
the
obtuse flute he'd
long wanted, blew
across the end of it
sticking
up... Blew across its
opening. Blew as if
cooling soup... Someone
behind him blowing
bigger
than him giggled,
muse whose jutting
lips he kissed as he
could... "Mouth that
moved my mouth,"
he
soughed, hummed it,
made it buzz... Hummed,
hoped glass would break,
walls fall. Sang thru
the
cracks a croaking
song
to end all song,

tongue's tip seeking

              the gap between her
            teeth, mouth whose
              toothy pout made
                              "mu"

        tear
      loose

                    •

      World release come
          down to his and
      her fracture, no bat-wing
          bones in her nose
                          but
          him aroused all the
      same, walls of an
          extinct retreat no
      more than ember,
                          his
      own flared, filling with
                          snow…
          His hand on her waist,
            her hand on his, all
          in either's head,
      whichever, fetterless
            touch whose roots,
                              they'd
            heard, lay elsewhere,
      world they'd have been
          on their way into, taken
                              so,
      exhaust-colored snow
          along the street outside
      their window, room
                      they
          lay remembering
                          in

            •

          Clavicle spill spoke
      volumes, book after

book after book.
　Spoke with a
muzzle on its
　　　　　mouth,
called it music,
　partings more than
words could number,
　made myth,
　　　　　　"mu's"
equivalent, lisp…
Imminent departure
made more poignant.
Possessed, said all
　they could, stuck
　　　　　pins
in their tongues,
　not that they awoke
but that they were
　　　　　awake…

Anxious aubade. Abject
sun… Awkward beauty
　had it been theirs to
　assess, attend to in
　words, bled among
　　　　　the
sunlit, leaving, blurred
　　　　　sight,
　stabbed eyes made it
　more than they could
see… Awoke to a dream,
　dreamt return, dead kin…
Anyone's guess whose
　　　　　world
　it was, anyone's but
his. Thought of his
grandmother, mother,
　uncle, brother, aunt,
　anyone's guess but
　　　　　his
what world it was,
　　　　　"Drifter's

Blues" on the box again,
   them running in place,
   rotting plums glued
      their feet to the floor...
                              Bigger
   than grandmother, mother,
      uncle, brother, aunt,
   dreamt andoumboulouous
      advent, at whose
                              advance
         his collarbone spoke...
   Clavicle spill strewn in
      all directions... No
   more than a croon
                              for
      condolence, no con-
      dolence... *We lay on*
                              our
      backs whispered itself
         it seemed as he lay
      without sleep, adrift
   off Cantaloupe Island's
                              lotus
   coast

                    •

   Hardly begun, began
   would-be waking, not
      to be taken in by
      dreams, left off
   dreaming, better
                        to be
   numb they thought.
   As if it were comfort
called it all in their
      minds, all meaning
   only. So quick
                        bidding
   farewell it seemed
      they sought
   inoculation, never

done saying goodbye
  once begun, reach
                    though
    they would notwith-
    standing, finality's
      hand an abstraction,
      answerless, aloof,
                        hoarse-
      ness the note they were
    after, audible witness
    all but out of ear's
                        reach...

After the end. Before
    the beginning...
All at once they
    both wondered
which... Talked
              with
    their teeth clenched,
                        hard
      to say who said
    less, ansonance
    an uncut grit they
        ingested, jawsplint
                        walling
      their way. What had
    been won some
      crude inducement,
                    to
        have been otherwise
        available, remote...
    Stripped indolence
                    a
    dream he dreamt
he dreamt he woke
    from reeling, head
    a rotating hindrance,
                        hit,
    slapped hand pulled
      away pulled up
                in-

to it
BEGINNING WITH LINES BY ANWAR NAGUIB

—*"mu" sixteenth part*—

A boat that sails to
heaven on a river that
   has no end,   high above
all but the elect among whom
  we of late no longer
numbered. Ythmic ship
                  we
  stepped aboard, stood
    aboard, or so we
               thought…
    Said of it as if it were
    music, "So spoke the
                 singer,
so ran the song," long sought
  circle of breath, inveterate
                 boast,
"book" bound for heaven, hook
  without end… Thought
we saw the heavenly city.
  No sooner thought than
  what we saw stood only
               in
  thought… Lit city seen
  from an airplane window.
              Lit
city we descended on. Stick
             city
  lit by a saxophone reed, found
    wanting, measured by Malik's
blue horn, blown hope of
heaven… Fit venue we sought,
             saw,
  thought we
      saw

    •

Had heard what we he and
she made was an older
                    we...
So now seemed we who were
awakened were not awakened...
And he of whom dreams apprised her
held at bed's edge a boat made
                    of straw.
"Ship of state" she heard, all
    but inaudible, exegetic
    wind ruffling a dog-eared
                    book...
    Qu'ahttet boat atop a flagpole
it seemed, junkanoo dreadnought,
    debris borne aloft, shot sky...
    The bed was their boat, he
    reminded her, roused out of
                    sleep,
    awake to not having arrived,
    unrisen, "book" meant get
                    away,
run...   Plucked air, plumbed
earth, inundated island. Wet sand
    arrested all advance. Outside
                    the room
    remembered bits of him haunted
    her... Mouth, flexed forearm,
                    chest...

Fleet squeeze of hip. Steep tease of
    meaning. To have been done with
    all thought to coincide. "Ship of
    state" vested every tongue, every-
one's ambiguous wish, ubiquitous
                    mouth she
    recalled extolling, him putting
    his lips to her between-the-legs
                    lips...
A new man in his and her bed, a new
    woman. Each the other's his and
    her dispatch. In steep demise mouthing
    abstract scat, said they were in

                              Ska,
        ensconced where before they could ask
        they were answered, each to his and
                                      her
ambage, all against
                    one

He and she sat stacked row on
row, politics twisting their
    lips, an extended whistle,
    warble where they thought
                        to embark…
        As in Wrack Tavern they read
by ledge light, tilted back on their
    barstools, teetering, barely made
out what they saw… Talked muse,
                      told who he
    called muse the muse redresses, decks
      her in alternate cloth, draping her
                    hips,
    cut just below ass-crack, ass
absconditus, broadcast
                weft

·

So again sat wasted in the Long
Night Lounge, iterativity's devolved
address,   who'd lain on their
    backs wanting more than was
                                there,
    ever there, a blanket their
ostensible boat, stroked gutstrings,
                                islands
        underneath, ribbed ships...
    Taken aback by how beautiful they
        found it, blown away, drift
    we recalled as wrack chatter,
                            later
        dubbed loquat scat...
                        We lay on
        our backs looking out at them looking
    in, cigar smoke swelling the veins of
        our necks, the boat of which
                                they dreamt
    a dreamt we beyond our
reach

Manipulable hope turned endless
hover. Steeped intertwinement of
tongues an amended kiss the
world it made in the image
                              of.
Reconnoitering mouth, mouth
rummaging mouth, crimped circle...
Caught mouth. Extinguishing mouth.
Would-be quench... At mind's mercy,
                              meaning mind
without mercy, reminiscing what only
might've been. What where was left
                              left

        atless, unavailable, amiss,
"mu" irredentist
even so

SPECTRAL ESCORT

—*"mu" seventeenth part*—

Not exactly a boat or
    not only a boat…
Weathervane, boat,
    flag rolled into
one, furled spur
                    it
    fell to us to
unravel… What
    we'd risen above
      tiptoed up in
    back of us. Lipped
      hollow, big
                    blow-thru
    gust we roughed
                    our
    heads with, we
of the andoumboulouous
    brush… Bank of
                    shade,
      mouth of shadow,
    fraught mouth. Deep
      song's bucketmouth,
      Rubichi's caught mouth
                    moaned,
    dreaming's *ever after*
      intransigent, ultimacy's
    ruse made more obdurate,
                    "mu"…

    Chewed charcoal, spat
out pictures… Black
      lips, black teeth,
      black tongue…
                    Music's
    tease held at arm's
      length, hardly had
    any arm left. Better
      we took rocks for bread

than be led to
believe we'd be so
                    embraced…
As if such a place as
Lipped Hollow existed,
   what had been wind
a way of knowing's
                    blown
   imprint supporting
us, music's at, else-
   where, reached. What
had blown suddenly under
                    us,
   walked on, better *as if*
                    not

had been heard
from, hushed

                    •

   Crawled out of thicket
we wrongly called
   andoumboulouous ambush…
A cooling breeze cut
   the tips of our
                    tongues
off. Something hit our
   heads and our hit
heads hummed, curlicue
   winds caressing the
                    backs
   of our necks…
                    As if
   as if had nothing to
   do with it, depth and
deferred ipseity arrived at,
                    buffed
   heads bothered by drum
thumps, metal plates put
   where we'd been hit.
                    Caught
   light lit our heads with

               shimmer, rubbed rabab
            strings. Headshine,
               synaesthetized light...
         Each of us an O, each
                                    made of
            welded chrome. Lipped
            Hollow a place abstruse
                                    flutes
         took us back to. Undersea
            bubble it seemed albeit
         inland, miragelike,
                              buoyed,
      burst

                     •

         Wind rife with ghost-hum
      blew between the sheets
         on the bed we slept in.
            Flutes blew thru gristle
            where we touched...
                           Suppressed
      billow, blown bank, burred
         voice we owed blowing,
         holes cut on hollow
                           wood...
         I held back, slipped
            off by myself, stole
         away, haunted head
            spouting obsequies,
                              crawled,
            kept close to the ground.
            Some said I was dead,
                              some
         a dream of the dead gone too
         far, dragged feet leaving
      marks in the dirt those yet to
                              decide
      said said it
                  all

LAG ANTHEM

—"mu" eighteenth part—

Last call in the city
of Lag. We laughed. No
  one so much as budged...
Left elbow on the bar
                              rail,
    whispered. Not so low
no one heard, everyone
                              heard.
    Psalmed her hips' high
ride, the fall of cloth
      across her jutting
                              chest...
Monk's po metathetically
    spun, recounted one
    morning leaving Eronel's
lair. Light off the
                              water off
      to the right headed
    south, head inexhaustibly
    lit by the back of her
neck's remembered
                              sweat...

    Bullets flew, bombs fell
outside, century's end as
    andoumboulouous as
ever. We were the ground
        he said was as it was
                              before,
    runaway buzz, bud, bush,
    boat, book...
                        Iridescent fin,
      redacted foot...
Recidivist fish, irredentist
                              wuh...
    We coughed incessantly,
would-be religion, would-be
    return to what had

barely been. As though by
    that we sought a southern
                floor,
subfloor,   flared airhole,
    hoisted Stra. Across the
    room Ananse webbed us in
    eyelock, goddessness
              borne
by glimpse, prodigal mouthpout,
    glovetight, close cut of
             hair...
39 was what it was we
were in, "mu" no more itself
    than Andoumboulou, both,
'8, '7, '6 gone by unbeknown
             to
us

    •

    Paper-thin wall we called
a world and on the other
    side what. Dream whose
inducement one of us broke,
            woke
    up from weeping, more than
    could be made of it
    made of it, moiling
      bass telling what it
          would
    take to amend... Where was
the music we wondered soon
    as we got there, nowhere
    near the music's where
          were
    there such a where...

Lifted our legs, an arrested
    run we made look like
    dancing. Knees waist-high,
            slow-
motion run, we ran in

place. Moiling bass
made it more than we
could bear, cut short
of
arrival, named, it said,
no
such arrival… Stood what
we knew was lost ground,
stutter-step, stomped.
Atless.
Almost
there

———————————————

Newly arrived. Arrayed in
    rows… Plucked strings
    tolling the extent of
    our duress. Waved and
                with
heads bowed hummed, hardly
    a beginning, anagrammatic
                    sttra…

    City of Lag segued into city
of So That. So that we on the
    Not Yet Express rode ecstatic,
    rode but not rode so
        much as trudged, waded
                  in
stra-dust, wish's would-be
    star tramped under our
                  feet,
  calfdeep in
debris

Asked his name, he said,
"Stra, short for Stranger."
    Sang it. Semisaid, semisung.
"Stronjer?" I asked, semisang,
    half in jest. "Stronger,"
                            he
whatsaid back. Knotted
highness, loquat highness,
    rope turned inward, tugged.
Told he'd someday ascend,
he ascended, weather known as
Whatsaid Rung... Climb was
    all anyone was, he went
                            on,
want rode our limbs like
    soul, he insisted, Nut's
    unremitting lift...
                    Pocketed
rock's millenarian pillow...
                            Low
    throne we lay seated on,
    acceded to of late, song of
setting out rescinded, *to*
    the bone was what measure
    there was. *To the bone* meant
birdlike, hollow. Emptiness
                            kept us
    afloat. What we read said
    there'd been a shipwreck. We
    survived it, adrift at sea...
An awkward spin it all got,
                            odd
    aggregate. Occupied. Some
    said possessed... Buoyed
        by lack, we floated boatlike,
    birdlike, bones emptied out
                            inside.
We whose bodies, we read, would be
    sounded, *We lay on our backs'*
low-toned insinuance tapped,

siphoned into what of what aroused
us arrested us,   tested us
                                    more
than we could bear...
                              Loquat
highness's goat-headed look's
unlikely lure... Lore made of
less-than, more than he'd admit,
                              muse
made of wished-it-so... Ubiquitous
whiff had hold of our noses,
nostrils flared wide as the
sky. Gibbering yes, that must have
been how it was, what there
                              was
at all a bit of glimpsed inwardness,
buffeted cloth, bones in black
                              light
underneath... *To the bone* meant
                              to the
limit, at a loss even so,   eyes,
ears, nostrils, mouths   holes in
our heads a stray breeze made flutes
                              of,
rungs what before had been water,
bamboo atop Abakwa drum... An acerbic
wine dried my tongue, my top lip
quivered. "Perdido...," I sang,
                              offkey.
So to lament beforehand what would
happen... Rope what would before have
                                    been
breath

•

Whatsaid sip they lit Eleusis
with it seemed. Barley mold
   made them wince... Heartrending
sky, held breath held high
                     as a cloud,
   Hoof-to-the-Head knocked hard,
   no bolt from on high but their
   lips' convergence came close,
                      Maria
ruing the movement of ships...
   The sunken ship they at times
took it they were on   no sooner
                     sank
   than sailed again. Failed or
soon-to-fail form, sisyphean
                  rock,
   rough, andoumboulouous roll.
                 Serpent
   wave, serpent wing, hoisted rag
   snapped at by wind. Flag she
   saw he lay bound up in, insisting
     they'd meet again. Lag anthem
   suffused every corner, music
                 more
the he she saw,   we the escaping
   they, calling out names no where
                   we'd
   arrive would answer to, nowhere the
                  louder
we'd shout

       Dark wintry room they lay shivering
in...
           Late would-be beach they lay
     under the sun on...
           Sarod strings dispatching the fog
       from Lone Coast, fallaway shore
         they lay washed up on...
                          Their
      lank bodies' proffered sancta
                   begun to
        be let go, Steal-Away Ridge
       loomed larger than life. Extended
       or extinguished it,   no one
     could say which,   the soon-to-be
                         saints
        arrayed in rows at cliff's edge, our
         motley band uncomfortably among
        them. A school of sorrow seeking
                      sorrow's
      emollient, albeit seeking may've meant
       something more, older than seeking, re-
     mote coming-to, barely known, of a piece,
                        beginning
      they broke taking
    hold

... that there existed a scout of love from whose effects of grief no one
could escape ...

—Wilson Harris, *Black Marsden*

EYE ON THE SCARECROW

—"mu" twentieth part—

The way we lay
we mimed a body
of water. It was
this or that way
                    with
    the dead and we
    were them. No
                        one
    worried which...
    Millet beer made
    our legs go weak,
                        loosed
    our tongues. "The dead,"
                            we
        said, "are drowning
    of thirst," gruff
        summons we muttered
    out loud in our
                        sleep...
    It was a journey we
    were on, drawn-out
    scrawl we made a road
of, long huthered hajj
                        we
    were on. Raw strip
    of cloth we now rode,
        wishful, letterless
                            book
        the ride we thumbed...
    Harp-headed ghost whose
        head we plucked incessantly.
    Bartered star.   Tethered

                              run...
     It was a ride we knew we'd
     wish to return to. Every-
        thing was everything,
     nothing no less. No less

                         newly
        arrived or ancestral, of
        late having to do with
     the naming of parts...
     Rolling hills rolled
     up like a rug, raw sprawl

                              of a
        book within a book
        without a name known as
           Namless, not to be
     arrived at again...

                         It was
     the *Book of No Avail* we
     were in did we dare name
        it, momentary kings and

                              queens,
        fleet kingdom. Land fell
        away on all sides.

                         Past
     Lag we caught ourselves,
        run weft at last
        adequate, shadowless,

                              lit,
        left up Atet Street,
        legs tight, hill after
           hill after hill.
        Had it been a book *Book*
     of Opening the Book it
        would've been called,

                              kept
     under lock and key...

                         Hyperbolic
        arrest. Ra was on the

                              box.
     It was after the end of
     the world... To lie on

26

our backs looking
into the dark was all
there was worth
                    doing,
each the aroused eye
one another sought,
swore he or she
                    saw,
we lay where love's
pharaonic torso lay
deepest, wide-eyed
                    all
night without sleep...
                    "String
our heads with straw," we
said, half-skulls tied with
catgut, strummed...
                    Scratched
our strummed heads, memory
made us itch. Walked out
weightless, air what eye
                    was
left...

            Someone said Rome,
someone said destroy it.
Atlantis, a third shouted
                    out...
Low ride among ruins
notwithstanding we flew.
Swam, it often seemed,
underwater, oddly immersed,
                    bodies
long since bid goodbye,
                    we
lay in wait, remote muses
    kept us afloat. Something
called pursuit had us by
    the nose. Wafted ether
                    blown
low, tilted floor, splintered
    feet. Throated bone...

Rickety boat we rode…
                    As
though what we wanted
was to be everywhere at
                    once,
an altered life lived on an
                ideal
coast we'd lay washed up
on, instancy and elsewhere
                        endlessly

entwined

SONG OF THE ANDOUMBOULOU: 42

in memory of Glenn Spearman

What we rode was a book. We
fell out of it, scattered.
  The book fell out of my
  hand while I slept. Page
    upon page upon page
                nodded
    out on... Fell from the
           hero's
hand on the page I gripped,
  never to be read again
  or, if ever, only were I to
          awake...
Walked each with an arm around
the other's waist, weathered
  hell, heaven's andoumboulouous
  remit... Me the hero, we the
    dream come true I'd leave off
              dreaming,
    thin line between the dead and the
living dead no longer there, fanfare
  remanding the day, dawn's burst
  anticlimactic one or two hours
          in...

    So as to return we stowed a
    part of ourselves away. Felt we
    fell, found it sleep we fell
          into.
      A low moan altered endlessly
    braced us, broke our sleep,
    Nazakat and Salamat were
             there...
  I put a part of myself aside,
    sought light, loosely, shone
    like a halo, hupped, marched
         up
Unreal Street unstrung, strode
  across Atet Street. Remembered

Glenn remembering Frank remembering
John, heard voices, Nazakat
and Salamat again... Stra strut
                                    it
was we called it, crawled unbeknown
to us. Having long bid ourselves
goodbye, we begged off leaving,
                                    better
said or sung than done it seemed we
reasoned, leaflike the trembling
                                    skin
we strode inside... Torn cloth, we the
would-be thread lay in wait with
whatsay, more than could be seen we saw,
said we saw, more than could be said

                                    we
saw. One made-up step made it seem
like dancing, anomie's make-believe
ball, scratch of sand and of intimate
stubble, whatever of late went
for love on Lone Coast... It was an
island we were on, anabatic sand
                                    we
strode across, come to where, if
                                    at all,
we'd live again

———————————

So that B'Head called hard rock pillow,
   pillow book the scribbling we saw.
We lay on our backs, rocks cradling
    the backs of our heads, lay looking
                              up
       at the sky... Starlight hit us with
    headshine. "Sky, be the writing we
      saw," we begged incessantly, breathless,
all but out loud. We lay on our backs,
                           arms
     out at our sides, putative wings, hands
    palms up catching light... It was Arrival
                      we were
   in, suddenly so with a capital A, all
                       we'd
always wanted it to be, been told it would
   be... Falling from the sky, an immaculate
                      dust
  attending
sleep

•

Statuesque, beautifully unbent as
we looked on, arched, insatiate
   bodies in the shape of trees bent
   by wind on Lone Coast...
                            Shook.
We stood on stilts. Mountain wind put
   parts in our hair, we heard singing,
   backed by an armadillo-back
                        mandolin...
It was a tavern we were in, we were in
                      Peru,
   some sung-about vamp grinding corn
on a Cusco jukebox, some vamp-till-ready
   we sat suspended in... Lumbering
harps had their way with the backs of
   our heads, we held on, wincing,
                    sat
with eyes averted, scattered ashes coated our
   throats. Cough seemed all we could do,
we could hardly speak, not so much
   Peru now as Paris it seemed, a
                 train
   what it was we were on wherever it
was, a train whatever it was we
were on... In the city's insides
albeit we were in Egypt, high-breasted
   Sekhmet statuesque at the metro
                   stop...
Beautifully bent all ears to inside an
inch of hearing, said nothing, muse
                meant
   lost in thought. As we were, who were
   otherwise also made of stone, Sekhmet's
                  Mem-

phite rock

Premature rebirth, fake book of the
dead. Burned or embalmed cosmic
    body by default... Screen outside a
    screen inside a screen, dreamt im-
    munity. Said goodbye having
                              hardly
        begun... Sang with a catch in our throats,
        cough caught in our throats...
                                Sang to
    have been done with singing,
                              song
not enough

GO LEFT OUT OF SHANTIVILLE

—"mu" twenty-second part—

Say-it-again got hold of us, we
shook. Now neither Paris nor
   Peru was it we were in...
                         We
were in Jamaica, St. Ann's Bay, a
     parish peril had to do with, perish
we thought it was we heard. We
heard a music made of swoon, sway.
   Swing had its way with us as
                        well...
   An unanswered message on the
machine rewound repeatedly, played
   again, thin balm against what
   ravage would come. A sunken isle
                     it
    seemed we lay washed up on,
   adrift on the ythmic, no sooner
   up than gone, dawned on as
                  though
our new day had now come, "mu"
suffusing the otherwise desert air...
   In the moving cubicle it arose we
     were in... Right sides and
   shoulders, right sides of heads,
                 pressed
against the window and wall as we
   went left,   pushed by the
bend we rounded, large-arced
    embankment our departure
                 cut...

   Sipped sand, so long without
water. Lone Coast elixir, mouths
   drawn shut... Euthanasic lip-stitch,
loquat liqueur,   Oliloquy Valley it
                was
   we came to next...   We were
   each an apocryphal Moses, feet

newly fitted with sandals, we
   strolled, scrolls long thought to
be lost unrolled in front of us,
                              dubbed
   acoustic scribbling, skanked...
Tumbling water filled my head, I fell
   out laughing, sand so long the one
                              thing
met my lip. Two words, *One love,*
   kept repeating, an asthmatic wuh
whose we dwelled elsewhere, scattered,
      worldwide auction block...
   Cropped air, coaxed inhalation...
                              Music
   the breath we took... It was only
there we wanted to be, the everywhere
   we'd always wanted,   ours,
                              albeit
   only an instant, forever, never to be
                              heard
from again

SONG OF THE ANDOUMBOULOU: 44

Wherever we were it was a tavern
we were in, a bar we stepped up
to, ordered... Stood in front of
the jukebox, bartender at our backs,

                                    rapture

what before we thought ruin...
Whatever we rode it was a record
we spun, wilting strings addressing
us as we looked out from Shard
Café, low-lying mist obscuring

                                    summer,

Lone Coast... Every arrival outrun
by the image we had of it, begged
it be the where we'd been after, there
there be nowhere we'd rather

                          be...

Vibrating string held us together,
hostage, nubs what before were
fingers albeit we plucked at it
even so, a subdued drum pounding

                                    past

words, words' amanuensis... Packed up,
departed, booked... "Cold water
and dirt," a voice we heard sang,

                                    wasted.

Whatever we spun it was a drink we
took. Goatskin, ecumenical kiss,
runaway tongue, whatever we drank

                                    it

was a drum we struck. So strict a song,
so cerebral it seemed. Whatsaid or
waylaid, no one to say which, the Old Book
an occult, acoustic book... Black
jewel, black jaw, jammed embouchure. Blue,

                                    belated

horn. Heuristic straw... So simple a
song and so sanguine, centrifugal

                                    how it

grew, gouged-out side of a mud house,

                                    more

than could ascend again, sunk... High-
register cry to wipe the earth with,
    bumped and abraded, buffed. Roughed
we'd heard we'd be, roughed it turned

                                    out
we were, horns held high, heads back,

                                    eyes
tight, Struff Street promenade,

                        struck

            •

Bells and the children of Badawi, newly
    named people of Ba. A vast crystal we
stood inside looking out of, looked in
    to see what was to come. Lit wicks

                            lighting
it, hornlip led the way, Callous the
place we came to next. "String my
    stretched head, high notes make me
        wince," words to a song we heard
    sung somewhere in the distance,

                        a lone
voice regretting itself it seemed... "And
what would that do?" we heard B'Head
    inquire, melonlike, infinitely afield.
    It was the firmament's opening night.
    Everyone was there. Far-flung celestial

                            seed
patch, each and every rolled head's
    wish... Orbiting head, esoteric

                        body.
Recondite string I plucked, all but
    outright wept. It was the soul's
night out, no one within miles,

                        every-
    one within miles, the Soon-Come
Congress's debut... Everyone was
    laughing, everyone except me but I
    faked it, filled in as best I could...

                        In the
outer reaches feasting on fruit nowhere to

be found in the world we knew... B'Head's
Belated Melon Patch Epiphany
we
dubbed it, see-thru, sealed on
all
sides

A region of hills it was we came
to next. Horns blew the book we
rode skyward. *Parallactic Hinge*
    was an alternate book... It
                    was a
    book we would've, had we been
    able, moved on into Albert's
principality, rung. Putative
    realm, unanswered
    prayer... What, if not
                    where,
    it was was a balcony's
        railing broken free
    of, the sound of
        Portuguese guitar...

    It was an elevator shaft,
                        a steep
        leap, a step not taken, two
    spoons at stairway's end
                    were
    what rung
was

Others called it namesake serenade,
what we were caught in, Badawi's
new ool-ya-koo. Name no sooner
said than unsettled, it was a
                              night
in Ethiopia next. It was a night,
                              renamed
of late, in Rhodesia, the Right Reverend
Frank at our backs blowing "One for
John," endlessly taken one step
                              beyond,
  blue gnostic
loop

On the outside as many scarecrows
milled around as there were stars,
    coatsleeves out at the elbow, sticks
and straw showing thru. It was night
    number 1002, a night northeast
                          of
Lake Tana,   the Falasha letting
                           loose
    a liturgical moan, blue mantric
    breath, make-believe bell I shook,
pretending, sitting in…   Strangers

    we were called, sojourners, named
in Amharic, marked. It was a night
  of innumerableness, a night more
                       of
    name than number,   a night not
      enough even so… It was an
Eighth Day unendingness, more
than could be said albeit whatsay
                     never
    ceased, a Nine Night rite's night
    number nine. It was now a night
    farther west, south of Khartoum,
numberless night of counting stars, Night
    of No Twin. We stood in a circle,
                     shirts

    and trousers filled
    with straw

A thorn caught in the horn's
    throat... Chimeless, chimney-pot
gruff... Blister was the place it
came from, Callous the place
        come to next, say-it-again's
                                        last
    word amended, endless reminder,
                                        bent

    ears of the elect... Onset of
horns like a long-sought
    landing, acoustical bank
                        we
        suddenly stood upon.
        Parched floor we fell
    out across, crazed,
                        ana-
        coluthic, endlessly
                        dis-
    tended
squall

It was a night nowhere near where
we were. Eyes popped, no one saw
me... I bit my reed, it was a black

                                  cat
    bone...   All I wanted was to
    walk with an ushering wind at
        each elbow, a bead of blood
      poised on the bell of the horn's

                               lower
  lip... The world was only a dream I
    dreamt at a stoplight in San Francisco,

                           Radio
    Valencia just up the block,
  me alive
again

GLENN ON MONK'S MOUNTAIN

—"mu" twenty-fourth part—

Next it was Austria we
were in. Unexpected rain
soaked our shoes,
unexpected snow froze
                    our
    feet. A bitter book
    took us there…
                    A bitter
book in our stomachs,
    an aftertaste on
    our tongues, a book
                    based
    on another Glenn,
                    Monk's
Mountain not the Monk's we
    took it for. A book of overlay,
a book about death at fifty-one,
                            a book
    we lay awake at night reading,
        a book we read wanting
        to wake up from…
                    So it
        was another Monk's
Mountain we haunted. Sat
                    upside
it crosslegged, lotusheaded,
                    humphed,
    heads encased in crystal it
    seemed… Bits of straw like
    unexpected snow filled the
                        sky.
    Stars were bits of straw blown
about in the crystal we were
in, the rags on our backs a bolt
    of black, star-studded
                    cloth,
    the jukebox dressed us in
    gabardine, burlap, scratched

our skin with raw silk...

A bit of straw caught in my eye
   made it water,   water
                         filled my
   head with salt... Straw, ridden
  by water, filled my head, my
throat, my chest,   salt filled
  my head with sound. A sound of
                         bells
     not of bells but of pounded
    iron, the Falasha spoken to
      by Ogun... I played "Asaph,"
   the horn's bell a swung censer,
                     wafted
    scent the furtive sound I sought...
Liturgical ambush... Fugitive straw...
Limbic ambush... Nastic address...
   Pads and keys cried out for
  climb, clamor, something yet
                    to arrive
we called rung. Rickety wood, split
   reed, sprung ladder. More splinters
  the more steps we took... Rung
   was a bough made of air, an
unlikely plank suddenly under our
                    feet we
floated up from,   rung was a loquat
  limb, runaway ladder, bent miraculous
  branch, thetic step... Flesh beginning
   to go like wax, we sat like Buddha,
                    breath
   an abiding chime, chimeless,
                  bells
  had we been
rung

Knowing of the world it
would remain without
   them, they lay entwined,
  atavistic twins. Thick
                  weather
   crowded the room, thin
  limbs,   wood becoming
   watershed, stitchless,
                warmed
each other's wintry
           skin...
They lay entwined, asymmetric
  twins, each the other's
  long lost remnant,   each
  in what seemed like speaking
   mounted skyward, each
                the
   other's complement, coughed
  up a feather, watched it
            float...
They lay entwined, atavistic
twins, empty streets ran thru
  their heads, they lay on their
                backs.
  Dark what once had been lit,
  deserted city,   arrived but
   without what advantage might
              accrue,
came to where they'd been before,
  what there'd been before now
  no longer there... They lay
   entwined, asymmetric twins,
             swung
  tangent to one another's turning,
   whatsaid its indiscreet regress...
  Unarrested regret roaming the
   warmth and the smell of their
            skin,
  residue of heaven, his her
insurmountable ridge too high to
  be reckoned, Anuncia's wrecked

arcade unveiling joint flesh bunched
   under cloth...   Not not having
                                   gone
  not having gone far enough, not
                               not having
  known how far enough went, west of New
Not Yet,   night was a mountain
  looming high, too tall to envisage,
  Anuncia's wrecked arcade reconnoitered,
                                  reeled,

    whatsaided
  back

       •

A river they thought they saw winding
snakelike. Looked at from an airplane
  window, sun bounced up from under,
                              blinding
    white... Taken aside, I sat beside
    them, an aisle seat, same row,
    snakelike what up close would've only
    been water...   So now no longer
                              was her
name Anuncia. Nunca was the new one she
  took. Never to be seen again, twinless,
unentwined, turned away, went, her
                         straught
    body wound wavelike, never to be
    lain with again... Wound wavelike,
                        snakelike,
  looked at from ersatz heaven, having so
  lain recollected, began again to say
                     goodbye...

Said wait but to what avail might've said
  nothing, Nunca's raw kiss gone away
  as though winged... As we as well were,
    however many we were, so many dead
                     borne
  about, not yet without soul albeit
                all
but so

·

They lay on their backs looking
up at the sky treading light, lies
    put away they thought. Moist eyes
he'd have drowned in, likewise
    the wet of her mouth.
                       Took
    between her legs his want of
respite unannounced... A nonsonantet
    it was he dreamt he'd someday play
                            in,
an unstrung lute he'd someday pluck...

    I pulled him aside to say braids
unravel, a meddler to my chagrin.
                        "'So
    Night sits me down before...,'" he
                    began
    but broke off, knew I knew what came
next. "I sistren," I said, not yet knowing
    what I said, myself no more the he than
                            the
    she of it regardless... Regardless,
    I pulled him
  aside

Prodigal rift an aroused we tossed
off, I was what was left. Talk made
my lips move,   fishlike...   I was
the remnant I fought the feeling I
                                            was...
    So it was that countlessness turned
my head, made it spin. Two meant
    more than I could say.   I sat to one
side, beside myself,   mounting light
                                                    folded
    in at more removes than I could count,
counting farther off to the side than
even I was, number now beside the
                                                point...

    The Abdominal Two I was tempted to call
    them, off to my left looking out at
                                                the
world, belly's rub wrangled and again
                                                begun
    to flare

(brayed)

Something we saw we only said we
saw we thought at first, not saw
  but made believe we saw we somehow
     thought,   Nunca sat on a see-thru
  throne. Inside the room
              which
  was all window our legs gave out...
    An altar the floor seemed,
                   receding,
  fell away, fell from the knees
    dropped down on to meet it,
  chivalric, no longer there.
                  To
  want was to risk it, not no
  guarantee, see no more than say
                    made
so

It was a tale told many times over,
muttered under one's breath unintended.
All the songs had long been sung.

Might've been bass, might've been
   guitar, strung so tight we tore
wood from its neck... So that
                           what I
wanted was what there was, Earth a
                              ball of
   dust and water... All the songs
     had long been sung,   numb choir,
                           sandpaper

    coating our
  throats

II

FRAY

SOUND AND SEMBLANCE

—"mu" twenty-sixth part—

A sand-anointed wind spoke of
survival, wood scratched raw,
   scoured bough. And of low sky
     poked at by branches,   blown
rush,   thrown voice,   legbone
                                     flute…
   Wind we all filled up with caught
in the tree we lay underneath…
Tree filled up with wind and more
                              wind,
  more than could be said of it said…
  So-called ascendancy of shadow,
  branch, would-be roost, now not
   only a tree, more than a tree…

It was the bending of boughs we'd
  read about, Ibn 'Arabi's reft
 ipseity, soon-come condolence,
                        thetic
  sough. We saved our breath, barely
                      moved,
  said nothing, soon-come suzerainty
volubly afoot,   braided what we'd
read and what we heard and what
  stayed sayless,   giggly wind,
                    wood,
  riffling wuh…   A Moroccan
  reed-flute's desert wheeze took
 our breath,   floor we felt we
  stood on, caustic earth we rode
across… It was Egypt or Tennessee
                   we
  were in. No one, eyes exed out,
could say which. Fleet, millenarian
  we it now was whose arrival the wind
                     an-
nounced

•

Night found us the far side of
Steal-Away Ridge, eyes crossed
   out, X's what were left, nameless
      what we saw we not-saw. We ducked
      and ran, rained on by tree-sap,
                              dreaming,
chattered at by wind and leaf-stir,
      more than we'd have dreamt or
thought. We lay on our backs looking
up at the limbs of the tree we lay
      underneath, leaves our pneumatic
                              book,
      We lay on our backs' unceased reprise.

North of us was all an emolument,
      more than we'd have otherwise run.
We worked at crevices, cracks,
      convinced we'd pry love loose,
                              wrote
our names out seven times in dove's
                              blood,
      kings and queens, crowned ourselves
   in sound. Duke was there,   Pres, Lady,
      Count,   Pharoah came later. The
Soon-Come Congress we'd heard so much
      about, soon come even sooner south…
                              So
         there was a new mood suddenly, blue
                              but uptempo,
   parsed, bitten into,   all of us got our
share… Pecks what had been kisses, beaks
      what once were lips, other than we
were as we lay under tree limbs, red-beaked
                              birds
      known as muni what we were, heads crowned
                              in
      sound only in
      sound

SONG OF THE ANDOUMBOULOU: 48

It was a freeway overpass we
were on, an overpass east of
La Brea. There we stood watching
cars pass under us, desert
    flutes gargling wind at
                        our
backs, an overpass we stood
                 on
    looking west... What there
was wasn't music but music was
    there. Where it came from
was nowhere, we heard it
    nonetheless, not hearing
               it
    before put us there... So we
                    thought
but wrongly thought, wrong to have
    thought we could. There we stood
atop the world looking out at
    the world. L.A. it now was we
                    were in...

    Inside each car someone bore the
world away, each a fleeting guest
    whose going we lamented, kin we
could've sworn we saw... It was
    a bridge over the river of
                 souls
    we were on. Lower than we thought
    we stood we stood looking, eyes
    all but shut by glare... It was
a river never stepped into less
    than twice. A river of light, it
                 was
a river of lies we were told, the
    biggest we'd outrun river's end...
Where we stood was a ledge beneath
in-between feet. Elegiac traffic
                 ran
    endlessly away. Our one resort, it

                                        said,
        was a lie… A glittering rung it was
      we took it we stood on, strung light
      filled with grit lit by sunset, soon
   to be remembered rush. It was twilight,
                                          the

        river was headlights and taillights,
        flowing both ways
      at once

                      •

        Head of echoic welter. Head I was
      hit upside. Curlicue accosting my
      neck, ears bitten by flues, fluted
          wind, Stra hest…   Head I was hit
        upside, a glancing blow. Whirligig
                                    and woe
          more than any one head imagined. Not
        that I saw much but that a glance was
          enough, one glimpse all it took…

      Head I was hit upside. Curlicue wind
          filled with rasp and chatter, all
      unquiet, back and to the sides and
          front… I stood on the overpass
      gazing out as did the rest. A caravan
                                        of
          cars, busses, trucks went by below.
        A congeries of trucks, busses, cars
          bemoaned Anuncia, her name now
                                        Nunca,
        borne away inside each one…   Head
      I was hit upside…   Branch I stood
        held up on…   Ledge, putative loquat
          limb, east of La Brea…   Branch I
                                        was
          hung up on…   The bending of boughs
          was a blending of eyelessness and
        light,   mending, my head was a host,
          B'Hest its visitor, lost in desert
      nearness otherwise won. Blinded by

the glint of the sun, her glimpsed
                              eye-
tooth, the bending a being flutelike,
                                   pitted,
    pathic, put upon…   Head I was hit
    upside, late Lone Coast reconnoiter's
      behest, distance's insinuative
                              light…
Swept and up to one side, hum inside my
      head's acceleration, breath blown on
    transverse flutes the floor I stood on,
                                   steadied
    me it seemed or so I dreamt… B'Hest had
    me sit, sat me down on the sidewalk, sad
    come to it so
soon

B'Hest had hold of us, no
escape. Not moved if not by reread
   meaning,   moved, music now,
                                 we
saw, beside the point... Late
   awakening, late arrival by hooklight.
Late feeling I fell back on. A bit
   of blood was in the wind, *rugs*
                             burnt
   Persian red, ash in the air
                        again...

   Wife dead, daughter's father's hand
bloody, not to be called husband we
saw... Abruptly back from thirty years'
distance, glimpsed ember gone out again
                             on.
   Something we saw we didn't see we saw,
     B'Hest held it, love's late recension
                        we
   saw...   Reminiscent autumn, reminiscent
fruit. Anuncia's proffered loquat, mouth
   an hermetic pout, Anuncia's mouth
                        perfect,
    pillow-talk
   sweet

•

Spark might've been ash that
spoke or might've been spooked, a
mango seed the size of an open
                              mouth
    in the middle of the street,
    seed I saw sitting curbside
    covered with dust and soot,
                              run
over how many times who could
                              say...
As if no longer on the overpass
    now, as if on the freeway, ran
from a runaway B'Us but it ran
    with me, a worm in the beak
    of the bird in the singer's
                              throat,
    Wemba's birdlilt waver not yet
    there though it would someday
    be. Something we heard it
    all but seemed we saw... Something
we'd soon be bereft of, B'Hest held
                              it
    as well, the imprint of crevice
    and curve the admission of cloth
    that we wore nothing underneath.
The admission of cloth's inexhaustible
    draw, spark long since dispensed
                              with
ignited, rough, incendiary husk... A
                              thin
    crease cut the wind, a cyst of
    emptiness, a mouth, a wrinkle
    witnessing what it remained to
                              be
seen. Thin impression of bones the
    admission of cloth that we were
    bodies underneath, stirring up upon
                              as
if by
    salt

Sat elbows-to-knees on the sidewalk,
sooted mango seed an opening, mouth
   a quick wind blew thru, blent

                              excursus
reading more than one way. Lure had
   to do with it, lurk had a say as
well, eye looked in thru and with
   as well blacked, glow gone beyond

                                 where
      one could see... Blent auspices,
   mixed emanation. Sirening fonio, helical
      whir. An underlay seeded, seen, silhouette,
         outline of legs under Anuncia's

                                    light
   dress, light's late carnal display...
      Had lain how long, been run over how
many times, couldn't say. Lurk had to
   do with it, Lone Coast reconnoiter,
jackknife-splay silhouette a gloved

                                 hand
to the face, caress gone awry, Udhrite

                              embrace...
      Who when loving die came back amended *or
      were killed,* not-to-be-called-husband's

                                    hands
      in cuffs

Udhrite arrest echoed Udhrite
embrace but nothing stopped. The river
of souls rolled on and was us and
we stood watching. Legs looked at
                              from
     afar stirred up dust... The
     admission of cloth we were bones
          underneath went on repeating,
       see-thru boon, x-ray bounty,
                              peepshow
sun...   Later motes took the place
     of stars, heads we were hit
  upside turned inside out, outside
     farther out... Stood or before
                              we
       knew it were standing, a First
          and Future Church of the Mango
       Seed's late birth, stood, suddenly
                              standing,

     nothing
stopped

ON ANTIPHON ISLAND

—*"mu" twenty-eighth part*—

On Antiphon Island they lowered
the bar and we bent back. It
wasn't limbo we were in albeit
    we limbo'd. Everywhere we
                            went we
    limbo'd, legs bent, shoulder
    blades grazing the dirt,
                        donned
andoumboulouous birth-shirts,
    sweat salting the silence
we broke... Limbo'd so low we
    fell and lay looking up at
    the clouds, backs embraced by
                            the
    ground and the ground a fallen
                                wall
    we were ambushed by... Later we'd
    sit, sipping fig liqueur, beckoning
sleep, soon-come somnolence nowhere
    come as yet. Where we were, not-
withstanding, wasn't there...

                        Where we
    were was the hold of a ship we were
                                caught
    in. Soaked wood kept us afloat... It
wasn't limbo we were in albeit we
    limbo'd our way there. Where we
    were was what we meant by "mu."
                        Where
    we were was real, reminiscent
    arrest we resisted, bodies briefly
                        had,
    held on
to

                •

"A Likkle Sonance" it said on the
record. A trickle of blood hung
   overhead I heard in spurts. An
introvert trumpet run, trickle of

                              sound...
   A trickle of water lit by the sun
      I saw with an injured eye, captive
music ran our legs and we danced...

                              Knees
bent, asses all but on the floor, love's
   bittersweet largesse... I wanted
trickle turned into flow, flood,
      two made one by music, bodied

                              edge
   gone up into air, aura, atmosphere
      the garment we wore. We were on
a ship's deck dancing, drawn in a

                              dream
   above hold... The world was ever after,

                              elsewhere.
Where we were they said likkle for little, lick
   ran with trickle, weird what we took it
for... The world was ever after, elsewhere,

                              no
way where we were
was there

SONG OF THE ANDOUMBOULOU: 50

—ring of the well—

Fray was the name where we came
   to next. Might've been a place,
might not've been a place but
    we were there, came to it
                     sooner
   than we could see... Come to
so soon, it was a name we stuck
pins in hoping we'd stay. Stray
was all we ended up with. Spar
   was another name we heard
                  it
   went by... Rasp we also heard it
               was
    called...   Came to it sooner
  than we could see but soon enough
   saw we were there. Some who'd
come before us called it Bray...

Sound's own principality it was, a
  pocket of air flexed mouthlike,
meaning's mime and regret, a squib of
   something said, so intent it
seemed. At our backs a blown
                 conch,
  bamboo flute, tropic remnant,
             Lone
  Coast reconnoiter come up empty
but for that,   a first, forgotten
  warble trafficked in again even so,
              the
   mango seed's reminder sent to what
  end we'd eventually see...

            We had
  come thru there before we were
told. Others claiming to be us had
  come thru... The ubiquitous two lay
bound in cloth come down from on

                                        high,
hoping it so, twist of their raiment
                              steep
      integument, emollient feel for what
      might not've been there. Head in the
      clouds he'd have said of himself,
                                    she'd
      have said elsewhere, his to be above and
        below, not know or say, hers to be
      alibi, elegy otherwise known...

Above and below, limbo what fabric
intervened. Limbo the bending they
      moved in between. Limbo the book of
                                    the
        bent knee... Antiphonal thread
        attended by thread. Keening string
          by thrum, inwardness, netherness...
                                      Violin
          strings tied their hair high, limbo
          the headrags they wore... The admission
          of cloth that it was cover, what
          was imminent out of reach,   given
                                        what
        went for real, unreal,
                              split,
        silhouetted
      redress

•

Over the next hill we ran into
rain, were suddenly wet. The
   two who'd fallen in with us threw
      back their heads, drank it
   in. "No more shadow mouth,"
                                    they
         shouted, which was true, the
         mango seed was way behind us
            now. No tropic sweetness's mock
            proffer, it was north we truly
         were, circling counterclockwise,
                                    in the
            clear, close if not quite, lifted as
         we circled it seemed. A conjoint
            lowing emanated from the ground,
         chthonic voices mounted higher,
                                    skyward,
            Spite Choir, the chorale we'd heard
            so much about of late we took it
         to be... Hallelujah Hill it was we
            were now the near side of, an
         allegorical hill we'd heard we'd

                                    come
            to, climb, come away from forgetful,
               rummage whose underside. Some we
            met said it was only a trap, rapt-
            anagrammatic diminution we were
            shadowed by, mango seed retreat
         notwithstanding, demiurgic trick...
                                    We
            paid them no mind, plowed ahead, un-
         impressed. The two who'd fallen in with
            us led the way. It wasn't wandering what
         we did, we circled, an earthbound orbit

                                    wanting
         out we went up on, low Saturnian shout,
                                    rings
            we walked. The two who'd fallen in with

68

us led the way, mapped our way, no sooner set

                                          our

   course than they
were gone

•

From somewhere near the well we
heard singing, voice an unheard-of
porridge, capsicum and roux,
                                        "Shadow
mouth," it lamented, "shook my tree."
    More than could be carried we caught,
were whisked away by, movement the
one mooring we knew. Eyes tightly
shut, one tear squeezed out by the
    impending end, what we wanted
                                        was to
        endlessly verge on exit, angling
    out, tangent to circle's edge, on
    our way where we'd be the last to
    say... Let all edges converge, it
                                        seemed
we said, cut away would-be end. Shell's
    edge, knife's edge, pearl we'd be
prompted by, refugees from where
    likewise last to say... It wasn't
wander what we did, we circled. Frayed
                                        at its
    edge though it was, wheel of soul, verge
we were driven by... Verge that we wanted
    verge was the song we sang had there been a
song we sang. No song left our lips.

    Nonsonant, we rounded circle's edge,
nonsonant ring shout, verge our muse
    and mount. Verge that we wanted verge
we bordered on singing. No song left
    our lips. It wasn't sing what we did,
                                        we
    circled. Song was the porridge voice's
privilege. "Shadow mouth," it repeated,
                                        "shook
my tree..." Sparks rose near the well, an
    extinguished fire, hung like a signal
    or a sign of moving on, a symbol, some
    said, showing forth... "Post-ecstatic"

was
a word we heard, "copacetic" a word we
heard, "After ecstasy what?" a question
posed in smoke… It wasn't smolder what we
did, we burned wanting verge,   verge
riding

our legs, we
bore thru

•

Verge that we wanted verge kept
insinuating,   song we'd have sung
    had there been one,   anthem
circling assumed. It was a healing

                                    song
    we sang had there been a song we
sang, swirling water we intimated
    wet our feet... Momentarily two, I
levitated, hoisted by thread Ananse-web

                                        thin...
    Wholly elbows and shoulders I was, it was
Nudge I knew I was in...   Pulled in
    early, a taste in my mouth I wanted
out, threw back drinks hoping to
    wash it away. B'Hest tended bar,
tilted my head back again and again.

                                    It
    wasn't the buzz but the feel of wash

                                        I
wanted. Water would've been enough...
Elbows and shoulders got forearms,
hands, lifted drinks. Water by itself
    would've done... Powder coated
    my tongue, I spat cotton. An
astringent puckered my cheeks,

                                an
        aftertaste... Limped, went limp,

                                    down
        and up at the same time,

                                    first
and forever bone-to-be-gutted,

                                break-
    intimated
flight

Tore the earth and tore the air
we heard later, we the instructive
two they went on about so. Tore
their throats wanting to swallow
the sky, tore their clothing,
                                        word
reached us farther along the way
they'd been brought back to earth,
                                                        now
            no longer sure they'd ever left…
            Tore their hair, wrung their
            hands, felt Ogun in their grip,
                                        tore
                skin. It wasn't limbo they were
                in albeit limber their legs and
                arms got, loose the realm they'd
            move thru next… Tore antiphonal rope,
                                                        hit-
            upside-the-head welter, gangly the walk
            they now walked. Legs made of sea lurch of
                late, tore the sea, we the weight on their
                                                        backs

        unbeknown
        to us

SONG OF THE ANDOUMBOULOU: 51

—cargo cult—

Took the wheel, put in a cassette
and we pulled out. We bid the Inn
of Many Monikers goodbye, pulled
                            away
   wanting never to come back…
   Nunca was at the wheel, namesake
     chauffeur we made-believe
     we believed in, stiff-backed
       ecstatics that we were…
                       Something
    new was on the tape so we perked
   up. What we heard stole tone from
   arrival, the where we'd eventually
be. It wasn't limbo what we did,
                   we
   sat up straight, backs ironing-board
                     stiff,
   not limbo where we were, a kind of
   loop we were in… It wasn't lost we'd
   have said we were, we reconnoitered,
                       Lone
   Coast itineracy long since understood,
   iffed and averred, we called it verge…

We were inland. Crab amble called out
from hills we saw in the distance,
   implicate sound sewn into Nunca's
   cassette… Morning light lit the
                    plain,
   a boon to the yet-to-awaken. Verge
gave way to green, green que te quiero
   verde, Spain it suddenly was we were
    in… No sooner Spain than it was
   somewhere known as Adnah we came to
                    next,
   everyone went around on all fours. Animal
   surmise local parlance proclaimed it.
No sooner were we there than we moved on…

Erstwhile Anuncia was at the wheel,
       albeit
of what began to change. What had been a
car became a van became a bus ad infinitum,
         an
 ambulance whatever it otherwise was, wounded
           crew
  that we were, an ambulance notwithstanding we
 sat up straight... We rounded the bend and what
 we wanted was there, satiety's rival tone a
rendition of soul we were slow to accept...

Leaned inward, sat up straight, crab
auspices' outward list compensated, Nunca's
 demiurgic wheel Anuncia's long remembered
  kiss gone south... Crash we'd have
 remembered gone blank... Anansic
        bend
 we'd have been caught in, webbed
         had we
 not leaned
in

And so withstood it. Stood, insofar as
   we stood, where standing flew into
  welter. Braced, borne onward, up, sat up
    straight. Nunca was at the wheel…

                         Never
   so much as made eye contact, never took
her eyes off the road. Never turned her
head our way or acknowledged us, never,
not so much as a nod… We sat in back. It
    wasn't passengers we were so much as

                        cargo,
  stiff-backed ecstatics though we were, that
   we were. Nunca, eyes glued to the road,

                       was

   also cargo. The road, eyes on it as
 they were, was
  all there
was

•

A dub cut came on the tape, took us
back to Adnah. A curve taken too fast
   took us out... Tossed out of the car,
  we ended up on all fours, moved
                                    crablike,
      sideways, forward, back... It wasn't
                                    limbo
     what we did or inverse limbo, bent
forward albeit we were. It wasn't limbo it
was or wasn't we were in. On all fours
      we rummaged around among earth smells,
   burrowed, buried our heads in high
                                    grass...

      The curve that had taken us out stayed
         with us. Centrifugal drift pulled us
         every which way. Bass got the better
            of treble, treble bass, reverb rubbed
      it in... It wasn't, looks notwithstanding,
                                    helter
      skelter. Crab auspices had worked out a plan...
                                                It
wasn't innocent animality we sought or asserted, no
   exemption unencumbered our way. We scraped our
knees and the heels of our hands moving crablike,
      movement seen seconds before so quick it
                                    seemed,
      movement we recalled from Lone Coast... It
         wasn't limbo we were in or that we limbo'd
   our way there, wasn't that it was or it
                                    wasn't.
   Crab Alley's outer precinct it seemed,
      nervous tether, dub echo's anansic net...

   It wasn't spiderlike or spiders we were,
      net notwithstanding, not eight legs
we had, only four... It wasn't spiders we
                                    were
      down on the ground like, it wasn't we were
                                    children

at play. We were on all fours greening our knees
and the palms of our hands on the lawn we were
    on, had it been a lawn we were on. Heads
in high grass, it wasn't a lawn we were on, it
    wasn't we were children again. Vibration got
                                                the
better of shell, we shook, scurried, tether rubbed
                                                reverb
    in… It wasn't roots we were after, we moved
        sideways, crab auspices' back-and-forth
        behest. We were on all fours encased in
        crystalline light, root like swine
though we did, our noses in the undergrowth…
                                                It
    wasn't horses mounted by loas we were, we were
                                                crabs,
nose around like swine though we did. It wasn't
an epic we were in, nose around though we
did, it wasn't that it was or it wasn't…
    Morning light bounced facet to facet. A
                                        beveled
    glass it might've been we
    were in

•

Millenarian drift invaded Nunca's
cassette. Whatever it was we rode we
   dozed off in,   peripatetic bedroom,
    hospital ward,   belly to belly
  on the seat farthest back the
                                incendiary
    two we were motored by… Morning
    light lit the way and again it
  was gone, a ghost what before had
  been solid, crab auspices' endowment
                                 up
  in smoke. So set the stage for again setting
    out, finger and ring to one another the
  two who lay sleeping, ideal we who awoke
    lay taken from… Merciless the loop we
                              were
    wound in, dreamt and utopic Two the
  arrived-at One we were leaving for. Tape
rolled and we rolled with it. Nunca was
    at the wheel, we sat in back… All but
    as far back as the two we were motored
                        by…
    It wasn't we were what they were dreaming
                           or that
  they were dreaming, wasn't we were dreaming
    them. No "it was" was at the back of our
    vessel, no unraveling… The two who lay
    entwined farthest back lay without dreaming.
    It wasn't that it was or that it wasn't.
                    No "it

  was" could be made of it, pure
  dispatch

To ride was a well gone to too often, a
dry world we circumambulated suddenly
awash, Anuncia's belated largesse.
                                        The
road was all there was and ride was all
we did. Curves and bends kept at us, we
                                        giggled,
giddy anyone was
at the
wheel

SONG OF THE ANDOUMBOULOU: 52

Never not another bridge to
cross, not before then so
  stark. We were beginning to be
    dead it seemed. Sought
                    silence's
    counsel, wise in that way,
      leaning toward light,
    off-balance... Had it been a
      boat we'd have gone under,
                        a
car we'd have slid into a ditch...
    It wasn't riskless we imagined
  we'd be but not defenseless. A
    feather broke our fall. We breathed
in... Light met the moment we left
                            left us
      breathless, lidless, looking up at
      the sun. It wasn't ecstasy as yet
        but we kept hoping. A feast
        had been set we'd been told...
    A token rope let down from the
                            sky
      hung out of reach and began to
                            unravel,
    wind what we took to be rope...

    On Lone Coast we'd seen a runway
of sparks, light bouncing off
    water, the sun itself drawn
  out, reflected on water... A
                        carpet
      of sparks inviting flight...
      Rung wound in with rug, lit
        runner... Auspice we took it
                        to be...
The bridge we began with vanished.
If not a runway and a rug it wasn't
    there. No way could we have walked
    it. We wanted it even so. A bed
                        of hot

coals it would've been, carpet of
                                    scars…
    Bridge being what it was, we turned
      away. The two whose future we
      were stood at our backs, each the
          other's whispered regret… "Locks,"
      he announced, lifting his hand, touched
                                        her
      hair, braids he saw lifting the boat he
    lay down in, course he'd have run, boat
    being soul. Twisting a braid with one
hand, she answered, "Hair," as if correcting
    him, locks' lifted boat rescinded, her other
                                        hand
      addressing his thigh… There we stood feeling
        the buzz of it behind us, turned away not
      knowing where we'd go next. It wasn't avenues we
      lacked, outlets abounded. Avenues availed
all around… None were so lit as the bridge we
                                        turned
      away from. Light's white gleam wove no rug
      on water… No such whisper of soul tugged
                                        our
    feet

Lift and being lowered he meant by
    locks, hair he knew to be hair
notwithstanding, hers the knotted
    highness whose equation lay
    concealed, boat equaling soul
                                    equaling
    body's low blow, below-the-belt clasp,
                                    clutch...
    The high inside of his thigh, quick
    sophic hand hers the hand whose caress
        came unexpected, the old story's
        echo at our backs as we retreated,
                                    buzz
    and bridge made us run. The old story
        echoed again, more than echoing, meat,
        breath, bone's buzzed arrival adumbrated,
                                    soon
    so abruptly come... What began as a bridge
now hummed in back of us, mixed ratteen voices,
        his and hers... It wasn't echoing an alternate
        life or a nether life, a stretch of lacquered
                                    rope
        wielded sticklike though it was. It passed
        from the back to the front of us,   a baton,
                                    rotating
        bone

•

A rug of white light on the bay, late
sun. "If by the end there's been a
    sign this will have been it." So we
        thought or said we thought, though
                                by the
        end there'd be no sign. It wasn't signs
    we were after, we sought what signs
        replaced, pitiless wish to be all
        there, that it all be there... It
                            was a
healing song we sang had there been a song
                                we
        sang, a soothing song, Wagogo we'd have
    been. A winding sound we'd have made
        had there been a sound we made. Zeze
                        bowed
        by raffia, mbira plucked by thumbs,
        a grinding sound we made had we
        made a sound... But by the end there'd
        be no sound, sign's mute witness
        rescinded as well, white rug's amalgam
                            of water
        and sun now neither water nor sun... It
            was a dream drummed into the air we
            took in, a brink we backed away from,
                                rickety
        bridge. Had there been a song we sang it was
        extremity we sang, all but strangling song,
                                a

    straining
    song

            —————————————

Brusque encumbrance unaccounted
for, bookless. Leafless the brink
  we stood on… Having been there
  the one vestige of soul we had
                              left,
    we in whose newly spun heads it
                            lay
    naked, a sheet of white light on
    the bay… Winter sun so unusually
bright but elegiac, brink was to
  book as rug was to water, debris
                          pooled at
    page's edge. Blunt circumference the
      brunt we ran up against, now
      sought solace leg to leg, rut
      comfort, amenity's insinuative
    touch… Locks were to lift as
                    weave
was to rope, weave's moot connivance
                         dreamt
   emollient, hard
stop

SOUND AND SENTIENCE

—*"mu" thirty-second part*—

Scales what would once have been
skin... Feathers what would once
   have been cloth... There that
claiming heaven raised hell, fraught
    sublimity, exits ever more to
                      come...
   A drum's head it was we walked on,
beats parsed out by ghost feet,
   protoghost feet our feet had
become. It was a dream of beaten
                      earth,
  beaten air, beaked extravagance,
   birds we'd eventually be. Albeit
feeling took flight's place, flight
    familiarity's run, movement found our
  feet, what once had been wood...
                    We
    stood as one, stung wood's revival,
 "Pinocchio" was on the box. Puppet
   run, strung wood, stump trumpet...
  Bugled admonition. Spun... It wasn't
                    swirl
  we wandered into, circling wind we
  considered moot, a way we had of
running in place... Phantom limbs they
   were we ran on, ghost feet that
they were. Nubs that'd once been feet
  lost their numbness. Feeling it was
                  made
us run... It was feeling's return we
  ran with, irredentist earth beneath
  our feet felt good. Irredentist earth
   fell away from our feet as we kept
  running, ran from day one long before
                  day
  one, protoghost entourage... Leg anthem
  the music intimated. "Spooks" it now
was on the box. We were anything but

there though not elsewhere, ythmically
    elect but loosed even so, earth a
                                        dream
  of drums come
  true

                        •

    It wasn't puppets we were, strings
tied to what had been wood notwithstanding,
    wasn't we were wood anymore. Runaway
earth abrupt cut from under... Ricochet
    and Reach rival names we knew it
                                by...
    Blinked and before we got there were
gone, protoghosthood its own haunt...
    So that Run it seemed it was we came to
next, a place, had it been a place, made
                                of
whisk, borne-away whatsee, blur... Blent
    vista such that splinters reared up
and walked, went remitless... Endless
    reconnoiter, endless vex, revisitation.
    Endless hoist and hoofbeat limbed on
                                high...
        Comings and goings not gotten over.
    Death not gotten over, goings away
        glimpsed again had us gone without
    going,   on to the heard-about
                                City,
  sounded
  out

El Suspiro del Moro, "the Moor's sigh," is the name of the last pass from which Granada is still visible as you go towards the sea. When he was fleeing, King Abû 'Abdi-Liâh (Boabdil, to the Spanish), the last of the Banû Sarrâj, heaved … a sigh of despair at this spot, as he gazed at his city for the last time….

—liner notes, *El Suspiro del Moro:*
Cantes Antiguos de Andalucía

SIGH OF THE MOOR

—"mu" thirty-third part—

Sat watery-limbed at the rhythm
table. Nommolike legs and arms
jointless, jooked oud everywhere,
ambient, jooked oud piped in on
    all sides… They were adrift
                    in late
ghosthood, protoghost remit, readied
   their way with string-stir, tremor,
                      plucked
   insistency, strum. Strewn aegis, abject
auspices, Anuncia no longer lost…
Her spread legs announcing children,
house behind a fence, mortgage due
   third of the month. It wasn't
                  astral
anymore, it wasn't cosmic, nightsky
   starless under smog if not bomblight,
   balm sought skyward sunk… It
               wasn't
Gilead where they were, it wasn't
Gethsemane. Flat realm, no rise,
   no resonance, booklessness the
   book they thumbed… No biblic
                aura,
no alternate life, at last they were
only where they were. Far from
Lone Coast, dreamless even dreaming,
   dreams no longer steeped in salt…

This the air grew thick with.

                             Oud-strop
leavened it all nonetheless. Tapped at
   the séance table,   knuckles, had

                       they

  had them,
          numb

        •

Why oud music arrived in the room
neither he nor she knew. Why Granada
  glimpsed in retreat flashed before
their eyes neither one of them knew.
                     Boabdil
  tapped at the table, tapped as on the
    wood of a guitar, palm to palm
  clapped keeping time, let go of
                  time…
This they nowhere near began to know.

They sat up late holding hands at
the kitchen table, lights out, candles
    lit… Susurrous air notwithstanding,
  they were only where they were, endlessly
  inflected sough notwithstanding,
                sigh
    upon sigh upon sigh… Sat ever so
  unknowing, unaware they played host.
                  Only
    the song knew, the song said, sang of
itself, an exclaimed "ah" choked on,
    swollen, welling sigh, sang of their
    unwitting relay… Southern Spain,
                southern
California, by oud-light lately the same.
  But they were only where they were,
heaved and exhaled, other than where they
                were

  though they
were

Sought their shadows in heaven,
nowhere near come true. Only
having to do with him thinking
them stuck there, not to be believed
outright... Thought them stuck
                                    but for
the oud's invitation, getting old in
the same place already old in the
same place, strings plucked with
an eagle-feather pick... Sought shadow
seen or sensed in heaven. Boabdil's
                                    resuscitated
sigh... They sat up late dreaming they
lay on their backs looking up at
stars, roof borne away by candlesmoke,
                                    roofed
amenities' eventual
demise

•

Beneath a window overlooking Lone
Coast, the sound of waves pounding
salt on the eardrum, a dream of
exegetic sleep. Unbooked but for the
    water's ripped edge, frayed page
    the rotating earth turned,   tore,
                                    one

    would someday see… So spoke the
    oracle, the exegete, dream of
a ceased read read endlessly,
                          read
      annulling omen's end…

Smell of salt on the wind off
the water. Sounds from the
                        amusement
park… A stone's throw from Lone
Coast no matter how far from Lone
Coast, the otherwise bookless
    two… Not that a ghost was
    there. More that where they
                   were
was a ghost of itself, Boabdil's
    abdicated kingdom equated with
latency's alternate run… So
    wrote the exegete, spoke
                  without
speaking, a stick's tip on sand
                  what
writ there
was

It wasn't that all things pass,
love not least among them, wasn't
that it was theirs once, wasn't it
no longer was. A zambra was on the
                                                box,
    love's unanswered moan, Moorish
      tiles evoking rendezvous, romance,
    walkway to Nunca's door... It was
        not never having been there,
                                        never
      it having gone, Anuncia's once
        what now was Nunca's, not not
                                            having
          known
        before

SONG OF THE ANDOUMBOULOU: 55

—orphic fragment—

          Carnival morning they
were Greeks in Brazil,
     Africans in Greek
disguise. Said of herself
                              she
          was born in a house in
heaven. He said he was
     born in the house next
door... They were in hell.
     In Brazil they were
                         lovebait.
          To abide by hearing was
     what love was... To
     love was to hear without
looking. Sound was the
                         beloved's
          mummy cloth... All to say,
said the exegete, love in
     hell was a voice, to be spoken
to from behind, not be able
     to turn and look... It
     wasn't Greece where they
                              were,
nor was it Benin... Carnival
morning in made-up hell, bodies
     bathed in loquat light, would-be
song's all the more would-be
     title, "Sound and Cerement,"
                              voice

          wound in bandages
     raveling
               lapse

               •

          Up all night, slept well
past noon. Awoke restless
     having dreamt she awoke on

Lone Coast, wondering
afterwards what it came
                              to,
   glimpsed interstice,
                                 crevice,
      crack... Saw her
   dead mother and brother
pull up in a car, her brother
   at the wheel not having driven
   while alive, newly taught
                              by
   death it appeared. A fancy car,
                                    bigger
   than any her mother had had while
      alive, she too better off it
appeared... A wishful read, "it
   appeared" notwithstanding, the
   exegete impossibly benign. Dreamt
                              a dream
      of dream's end, anxious, unannounced,
   Eronel's nevermore namesake, Monk's
      anagrammatic Lenore... That the
      dead return in luxury cars made
                              us
      weep, pathetic its tin elegance,
                                    pitiable,
         sweet read misread,
         would-be
      sweet

SONG OF THE ANDOUMBOULOU: 56

At long last we came to the
Dread Lakes region, graduating
body and bone. It wasn't we
so much as web we were, buh,
                           the
   implied increment, zuhless,
                           web,
    no zuh, no buzz... Got there
at long last thru a maze of
   cities, quaint faces arrayed
on balconies along the way.
                    Matted
  hair dotted the ground as we
strode in, the earth itself quick
   with feeling, sentient,
                  felt
    it rub the soles of our feet...
It was a march we were on, a
   campaign, carnival trek
translated of late and of late
   what before had been ruse
                 become
   real. It was a float we were
on it appeared, a layer of light
between the ground and the soles
   of our feet... It wasn't we were
                 prey,
buzzing fly, flying fish,   wasn't we
were inside Ananse's web, Anuncia's
net. Web it was we were, it wasn't
  we were caught. It wasn't we
were web's, we were web...

                  Invisible
lips blew ripples on the water, vatic
  breath blown wordless, the exegete's
bequest, endlessly expended wind. The
                 lakes'
   faces fraught with import, splay
auspice's day begun. Day wet with

allegorical water, rebegun,
                                        endlessly
repeated, dreamt amendment's end, lakes
     looking back at us it seemed. Faces
we'd seen in cities we saw again,
                                   watery,
all but undone... It wasn't Babylon where
     this was nor its outskirts, dread
faces captive kin,   furrowed lakes
     where before they'd been featureless,
                                        blank
but for the exegete's bequest. Fraught or
     without furrows, Fret Lakes either
way, Dread Lakes all the same... Dread
Lakes lay southeast of everywhere,
endlessly down and to the right. The
                              farther
     they receded the deeper we were there,
apart from where we otherwise were...
     Got there in trucks or simply walked,
it wasn't clear. Dread Lakes had it that
                                   way...

     Dread Lakes lakes in name only rife with
names, names' unthinkable dearth. Fret
     Lakes, Dearth Lakes, Dare Lakes like
bone, Bone Lakes' alibis... Lakes rubbed
raw by strung voices, parched earth what
                                        before
     had been mud. Mud what before had
        been water, Dread Lakes fiery dry...
     It was a furnace we were in, dotted
        bodies eventually blent, Dread
     Lakes' evaporative largesse. Blent
                              we
partly were. Web it was we were. Blent
                                   was
  web's distant
kin

•

The waterless lakes they turned out to
be turned us back. Turned away, we
   turned inward, buoyed against our
will, better to've sunk we thought...
Thought we thought, we admitted,
                              abstract
   baptists, glad to be dry, undunked...
An adamant canvas it turned out
   we were on, polychromatic
powders, dust. Dotted bodies
                        begun
   to be other than bodies, half-again
   themselves not themselves...
                              Kissed,
   otherwise moistureless, caressed,
   hands and fingers finding their
way. It wasn't grope what we did,
                              we
decrypted,   bulge and declivity were
                              code...

   Desert love, bedouin strand at lake's
edge, into it before we knew where. Signs
all around, how to read them none of us
   knew. It wasn't we were lost, we lost
   track absorbed as we were,   recondite
                                    recess,
   crevice, fold... Immersed in what wasn't
there, desiccant slough what was, toward
and away were now one. Code even
   so, siphoning substance... Dread
                        Lakes
   alias, cavewall inside out,   dotted
      bodies bespoke "immanent elsewhere,"
half-again "all but already gone." Why
                              we
   became web was no conundrum, why
   buh wasn't buzz no zuh... Pelvic Hollow

it was we now called it, come upon as

                                                  drift,

    dry
    run

Dried up if so much as looked at, dreamtime
equation of body and lake, down under
    lay intangibly above... We stood
on the lake's bed, what was left
                                of it,
    wished-for new beginnings no beginning,
    the new world we expected up in
smoke. Again gave thought to the
    he and she we saw embrace, etched
        andoumboulouous forms we saw
                                in the
    dirt, thought we saw Rorschachwise...
                                    Moved
    among landmarks whose names were
    legion, Rock-the-Spotted-Lizard-Passed-
        Wind-On, Fallen-Tree-Where-the-
        President-Spat... Ledge-Where-
        the-Bramble-Tore-Pant-Legs come
                                to last,
        color clung to our feet. Drift,
        aboriginal forage... Abject
        endlessness, abstract arrest... Color
    claimed our feet, drawn-out exit,
                                dreamt
        amenity, endlessly
    cathectic
trek

•

What would accrue to color kept us
afoot. Paints and pastels lay in our
   way... We the painted ones ran, feet
      wet, canvas rent. Blue rabbits
      we might've been... Namesake
                                    hair
      was what shrubs and brush were,
                                    the lakes'
      eponymous locks. Dread Lakes was
   the name it all went by, lake floor baked
   by unremitting sun, low scrub and brush
were brown. Scrub was what covered the
                                          ground
      and what we did, endlessly abraded earth
      rayed out around us, endlessly scratched-at
sky... Hedge-the-Judge's-Pay-Lay-Hid-Behind
   lay to our left. Withered-Creek-the-Wounded-
      Bird-Left-a-Feather-In loomed up
                                    ahead...

A sonorous canvas it became as we
advanced. Blown reeds accosted us
   with wind raising dust. Grit got into
      our nostrils, eyes and throats... An ill
      wind in the dead of August, blown
                                          reeds
      laid us out on a cooling board... It wasn't
   we were dead or that the world was, wasn't
      we bid anything goodbye. It was the
      all-in-all otherwise known as web and it
                                          relaxed
   us. Grit was web's alias, web in scrub disguise,
   scrub's atomistic reach... We made up ground
                                          in a
      made-up landscape, no less real for that...
      Wind on us hard as it was we ran even faster.
                                    Stride
was our true country, native
                        ground

Abstract canvas, earth tones notwithstanding.
Color clung to our feet. Caved alias, pelvic
   alcove, under intangibly above...
   Knotted highness lay on the ground
                                    in
clumps we tripped over, lakes and
   canals come to in dreamtime,
   intricate fingers braiding love's
                         true
locks. Dread Lakes it was nonetheless,
                              Dredge
   Lakes were it under lay visibly above,
  Dram, Drawn Lakes it was, Dread Lakes
   all the more even so. Dread Lakes was
  where we were, where we'd been, where we'd
  be. Dread was the color claimed our feet...
                                  Might've
   been saffron or something like henna, red-
  brown, yellow-brown, spiked earth at the
                                soles
  of our feet, heels and the
  balls of our feet
 pestling
light

A worked awkwardness ran us over. "We
don't care" popped out of our mouths. Stomp
got our feet, ran up our legs, trunks, necks,

                          put a
   big Foot up the sides of our skulls...
   Anticlimactic we called it, disconsolate,
paint put on us by the way we came
   thru, scrub's perimetric net. A step
short of web's edge, nothingness. More

                         than
   could be come to, caught. It wasn't
as we'd said, wasn't we were free, wasn't
   as we'd said about buzzing fly, flying fish,

                        wasn't
  we were wingless, web's it
 was we
were

DREAD LAKES APERTURE

—"mu" thirty-sixth part—

A wash of sentiment flooded frame,
ground, figure. The wall between
  "given" and "gone" grew thin, the
    dead surviving death in a swirl of
                    wind...
  "Children of the Night" was on
  the box. Wayne's nasal cry nudged
us on. We were them, their lapsed
    expectancy, gun barrel nuzzling
    the backs of our necks. "These
                   children,"
  we said with a sigh. Sat on grass
    eating something called poppin,
  sprung from an acoustic mirror,
suppositious canvas, prepossessing
  light... An elysian scene out of
                  childhood
    almost, except the children sipped
  beer, bourbon, wine. Spoke with
    mouths full, mouths wide open. We
saw poppin inside as they spoke...
                  Chuck
  E. Jesus they talked about going to.
  That or having gone, unclear which...
    Rude crew in whose childish guise
    our departed kin could again come
                  back,
these children were come-again elders,
  the elders were children again... These
children were drunk, dredged eldren, Drain
    Lake's namesake brew the beer they
    drank, drowned elegiac youth...

Light's bloom lay in disrepair, wounded,
lest it be called indulgent, earth prove
    overly lush. Sipped beer, bourbon,
                  wine,
  spoke with bubbles in their throats,

blew bubbles when they smoked
    instead of smoke. A meeting it
    seemed albeit angular, diffuse, a
                                    rogue's
way with aspect, flecked. A synaesthetic
                                     dance
they could taste, called it poppin, hop
invading tooth, tongue, jaw… A great
    gift it seemed, bubbletalk ascending
    as it did even so. Brass rallied abject
reed… Dawn's colors came on without
                              warning,
    children of the night though they and we
were. Light's bloom was back or it was
    we were light-headed, lit heads loose
                              in a

    dream of
    light

On a lit canvas what could've been
us, blown away. Was, andoumboulouous
   we, andoumboulouous they. Wasn't,
andoumboulouous both… What to
   say: there was a was, there was a
                              wasn't.
   The vehicle we boarded held both, blew
up. What to say: there was an us, there
was a them… The beginnings of
light, this was to say, abated, weakening
   glow begun to be said goodbye
                              to,
   flecked air fallen thru by motes…
Eye-squint, it went to say, went awry.
   "These children," we said, sucking our
   teeth. Newly come albeit chronic
                              elders,
      reached out, drew back less than what
was reached with, Nub it now was we
                              came
   to, tokens fell from the sky… Nub
                              was
      where we were, where we'd been,
                              where
      we'd be, chronic no
   less newly
come

III

NUB

SONG OF THE ANDOUMBOULOU: 58

The intractable two no longer among
us, he her ecstatic exegete, wishing
   the world away, nose between her
legs as in a book... Comes up for
                                  air.
She straddles his lap. A stiff bouquet
   opens their noses... Not that it
would ever not be there, not that,
      even so, it would be the same. Animal
grace fallen down or away from,
                               all
for naught if not amended, made of its
                                own

   remit. A lit screen showed it was us
   rubbed away, Dread Lakes' namesake
brew, drank our fill, poppin fell from
   the sky... Oddly fed. Feasted on
                          grief.
   Debris bumped our heads, rubble
hurt our feet. Fingerless, if not
   without hands, drew back from
                       reaching,
   Nub the new kingdom come...

Remnant light lay weakening light's
retreat, children said to be of the night no
   longer children, such what we'd have
otherwise been... Somewhere someone
                    chanted,
   an echo we looped and relooped. Dub it
   was as much as it was Nub we were
in, ersatz eternity looped ad infinitum,
                  loop
given reverb to. Echoes flew close to the
   earth, bleak reconnaissance. Tape ran
away in reverse, took us with it, beginning
   to be alive it seemed... We whose two
   demanded a longer count long since
                  riven,
   I was only what was left. She his unim-
   pressed interpreter, I thought, bone as

well as body looked at, leafed, eyes lit
                                    like
ember, book of no turning
                        back

                    •

    Back seemed all there was, alive
begun to appear to be ember, interregnum,
    deathroll exception, proof... Terrain
      like no other, nubscape. Flags
                            filled
    up the sky... Two loomed incalculable,
aggregate regress, Nub's raw republic
absconded with we thought, Nub short
    for Nubia we thought, thought we
                                thought,
    there no more the where we'd have been...
    Such that one, being what was left,
blew up, an eye before that a blind
                            lemon,
    blue lemon, teardrop adjournment,
salt... So that everything it took took
    wing, newly adduced or indifferent, no
one to say which, well-paved outskirts
    of Nudge notwithstanding, Nub's new
                                landing
    point. Armless, one lay in wait, moot
warrior, crouched behind a bush put upon
    by wind, misgiving, doubt... There
      that we'd have otherwise been, blue
    summit, state stand only as we'd allow.
                                Lovers'
dub covered lovers' republic. Something
obscene, it seemed, was on the box...
    Crawled on our stomachs, elbows to
    dirt. "The Inch Worm" was on the
                            box...
    The box filled with water, dry rot,
                                worm
    routes voices ran
                    thru

Wrung water from a sawed-off branch,
coaxed omen. Hollowed-out tree trunk
   thumped… So much easier said
  so much of what we said, rhythm
                      log
   wasted by ant wing, worm jaw,
                  balafon
   bridge undone. Scrounged around
among bushes and tree roots. Went to
  rise but our heads held us down…
We were Andoumboulou, bloated
   heads atop shrunken bodies, the
                 song
said to be ours a repeating head's
  vamp-till-ready, torn heads' mended
spin. Shrunken bodies, bloated heads,
                we
   were Andoumboulou, bodies more
   head than husk were song body, torn
                  heads'
  compromise

•

Rummaged around on all fours to
bug accompaniment. What we wanted
we couldn't have. Multiple the
names it went by, legion, wars
                              over
which one fit broke out, nation of
none though we were... Not yet
nation of Nub that we were, said to've
been born with barbs in our skin,
anaesthetic nation of Nuh... Said
                              to've
been born in beds made of glass,
                              "Bed,
be our balafon bridge," we exhorted,
"bed, be our rhythm log." Glass meant
broken, slivers where we lay, ythmic
                              digestion
held even so, shards bone-deep it
meant... Bridge meant see-thru,
sayless, something we'd assume
so elliptical it seemed, unsay said it
best... Unsay said what there was of
                              it
to say. Nub's low skyline lay to our
                              left...
Nub lay close to the earth... Nub cut us
off. We were never all there. Raw knuckles
pounding the dirt bled rivers. Bloodrun
                              carried
us away

•

Scrounged around on what earth was
left, the intransigent few Nub stubbed
    its toe on. All of earth was what
    earth was left so few we were, back
                                    at
some beginning it seemed... It was
    morning, gray morning, pearl divers
    chanting in the Gulf beside the
bed, clock dial phosphorescent, lit.
    The lovers lay again without
                                recoil,
    world without war without end
    intimated, dream they'd awaken
from... In a ship's hold helpless,
                                hair
the look of thicket, ship of state they'd
                                call
    it, crushed... But for now, before that,
    sleep of ages, again as if starting
from scratch. Asleep yet on the tips of
                                their
    tongues kept asking, salt not known to
                                call itself
    salty, what to
say

What of us wouldn't carry caught
    on the bank of the river, lit spear
  brandished on the bank of the
     river, lit spear hoisted, flung…
                                    Locked
      and braided eldren sang without
      sound, sang without voice with
  what blood laid claim to… Blood
    was a paperthin slick atop water.
                                    Water
ran where voices would've been…

    Blood spoke in tongues from the
       far side of tongues. Bed be none
    of the above, blood admonished,
                                    unsay's
        day if not begun
      soon
  come

SOUND AND CEREMENT

—*"mu" thirty-eighth part*—

Caught in coastal weather, came
    in from the rain, they the two,
we who will have been none...
    It wasn't an epic we sang had
    there been a song we sang, heroic

                              waste

    around us though there was. The
    beloved's long-distance voice
was what it was. Muse meant lost
    in thought it reminded us, erstwhile
    epiphany, snuffed... It was all

                              a wrong

    turn or we took a wrong turn. All the
    roads ran off to the side and we as
well, we of the interminable skid... We
    were they of the imagined exit,

                              he

    and she of the adaptable tongue,
    teeth, lips, mind's own sacred
    ass-cleft and crotch, we of the

                              exiguous

fit... Erogenous mind's dilated aperture...
    Cloth tore, ground gave way...
    World being anything but, we
    retreated, each the other's remnant

                              wisp,

    remnant caress kept only in sleep...

Fleet release the embrace made myth
of, arms' tight winding and wrap a
    kind of cloth, cerement the skin itself.
    A spun sound answered us inside

                              and

    out, revenant, runaway love the least
    of it, run though we did even so... The
    lost one's attenuated kiss was what

                              it

was, the beloved's long-distance

                                        breach
          and bedevilment, beckoning we broke
          loose from. There was fold on fold of
            cloth and it was us, caress claiming
              myth a burial of sorts, cerement the
          spin we rode rode us, raveling arrest
                                        un-
          done... A republic of none the one included
                                                us,
              no word to speak it with, dumbstruck...

              Beginning to be the end it seemed...
          Ending begun to be come to again. Ending
          going on and on... Wanting the world,
              what of it was ours not enough. The
                                        sun
              rose, night notwithstanding. Came up,
          hung deep in the wet sky. A kora's
              tight strings assisted it, launched it,
              held it for us to see. The sun was one of
                us it said. What it meant by us lay
                                        cloaked
              in peal, ping, fado, world wanted only
          for the sound it shook loose, Portuguese
                                        tremor,
              trill... What wasn't us we had no way of
                knowing. What it meant by us was
              unclear, us included so much, sun
                seemed an alternate cloth... Beside
                ourselves all night, no sleep. We
                                        were
          they whose bed was anything but. They
                                        lay
              awake in our sleep, we in theirs they
          intimated, a song of song's end had there
              been one, a broken song we'd have sung
                                        had
              there been
              a song

•

Reminiscing the wet of each other's
mouth, recollected their boned
embrace. In a hot room haunted by
snow, the intractable two
                              in
disarray... Borne away by who
knows what. Were it a bus, relegated
to the back of the bus... A politics
articulate of late of late let go, a
pool of remorse we fell into,
                                    it
might've been us in back...

                            We who
rode in front rode as well in disarray.
Time's raw inroad it was, it wasn't
a bus... Heaven it was we were in,
not knowing we were. Hell was not
                              knowing.
We were in hell... So it was in the
kingdom of Nub. No way could we
see past our noses. Dust got in
                          our
throats, noses, eyes, fell all around
                            us...
Dust was rub's accretion, Nub's
                          inces-
sant regress

•

Stark light the day I saw thru. I
too spoke with a shell on my
   voice, tongue a thick worm in
my throat. I was at the beginning
                          again,
   wanting to undo and redo what was
done. I was only what was left...
   Nub was being what was left, I
was Nub. Nub was being remnant,
   regret. I was debris, I was what
                       was
   left. I wore a mask made half my
                       face
   numb. One side hairless, the other
unshaven, talked, ate, drank
                     with
one side of its mouth, numb side
confounding what the quick side
felt. I was only what was left...
                    I wore
a mask made half my face grow
   stubble, stubble side scrambling
what the slick side felt. I was only
                       what
was left... Of late looked at from another
                       side,
   all sides... Out, over, either, both, I
                  was
  what was
left

———————————————

It was getting to be the end again,
day done up in black, night white,
　　edge along which we fell, thought,
　falling, this is what the songs all

　　　　　　　　　meant...
　　All the songs were ecstatic,
　　　　　　　　　lovestruck.
　Hearts bled... Violins... A worm was in
　my brow, bit me, heart's own target,
toyed with, I was only what was left...

　　Abbey Lincoln sang a Sufi lament.
　　Truth blurred if not blue, blue, bereft,
face never seen they say... Lookless,
　faceless, voice heard in hell, life love

　　　　　　　　　alluded

　　to lifted, love's
　　laryngitic
address

The vote came in early. We ignored
it. No ballot-box auction for us...
Nub's uninstructed dance's bare
   feet, music we took them for.
                                  At a
loss with only bodies to fend with,
   nonsonant waves kept coming,
sang without wind,   saltless,
     waterless,   Nub's inverted
run, Nub newly vented by horns
                           blown
   elsewhere, bells full of insect
   husks... Nonsonant scruff held
on to, sheerness... Nothingness
it seemed we grabbed at, gathered,
beginning to be unending it seemed.
                         We
   were beginning to be lured again,
ready to be hectored, huthered, move
on, beginning to be uprooted again...

A peppered expanse the country we
crossed. Space doled out so stingily
   we wept, love's numb extremity
the outskirts of Nuh, name whose
                      elision
   we embraced... A tale told many
times over, known before it reached
   us, known before we knew, un-
   backed alley of soul we wandered
                         into,
   shadowbox romance it was called...
Come of late to creation's outskirts,
rub's new muse a republic of none, a
   yet-to-be band the band we were...
We were Andoumboulou, dreamt
                     in-
   habitants of "mu," moored but
immersed, real but made up, so much
   farther flung than we'd have thought...

They the would-be we lay on a bed
the size of Outlantish. Lip attesting
　　lip, tongue rummaging tongue,
　　　　　　　　　　　　　took
　　between finger and thumb the hem
　　of her dress, flat bead of sweat, salted
　　　　　　　　　　　　　　　cloth...
　　A hammer hit them each on the head.
　　Hammered heads rang and rang without
end...　　Called it creation, called it
　their clime, close where there was otherwise
　　　distance,　　mute endearment,　　recondite
　　embrace... So much farther, felt even
　　　　　　　　　　　　　　　so,
mouth she remembered, home. His to hear
　　her tell it, hers were it his to say, whose
　　book was of lengthening limbs, hers of
　　　　　　　　　　　　　　the
　unquenchable kiss... A tale told over and
　　　　　　　　　　　　　　over,
　　long since known by heart. Lay belly to
　　back, turned belly to belly, each the other's
dreamt accompanist, music they made in
　their sleep... Frayed hem the interstice,
　　　　　　　　　　　　　　time's
　moot rule. Time's moot rule amended,
　　　　　　　　　　　　　　echoed
　advance it was
　also called

A first unfallen church of what might've
been. Let run its course it would have
    gone otherwise, time's ulterior bequest…
This they had a way of imagining,
                                    this
    they so wished it to be. Abstract he
    at the back of her mind, she at the
back of his, each the other's Nub
    constituent, ghost of an alternative
                                    life…
They were we before we were, ancestral,
                                    we
    who'd never not be ill at ease. A vocation
    for lack he'd have said, she'd have said
longing, a world, were they to speak, be-
    tween… What wasn't, they'd have said,
                                    went
    away, would come back, first fanatic
                                    church,
        what would
        be

　　　　•

They the would-be we talking talk of
election, devotees of Iemanjá. Glass-
green water they were in up to
　　　　　　　　　　　　their
shoulders, each the other's moored
recess… The way she said his name stayed
with him. More made of what wasn't
there than what was, whispered,
　　　　　　　　　　　　　came
back again… Love called out from side-
walk to balcony, rooftop to galaxy,
　　　　　　　　　　　　　　mute…
More made of what was there than
was there, mouths vow-heavy at
bed's edge, lip-touch never to be done.
Never to get up again it seemed, lay
　　　　　　　　　　　　shaken,
endlessly commemorative advent,
　　　　　　　　　　　　　dreamt
evanescent caress… A first unfallen
church it might have been. Let
run its course it would have gone
otherwise, time's ulterior bequest…
This they had a way of imagining,
　　　　　　　　　　　　　this
they so wished it to be. Abstract he
at the back of her mind, she at the
back of his, each the other's Nub
constituent, ghost of an alternative
　　　　　　　　　　　　　　life…
They were we before we were, ancestral,
　　　　　　　　　　　　　　we
who'd never not be ill at ease. A vocation
for lack he'd have said, she'd have said
longing, a world, were they to speak, be-
tween… What wasn't, we'd have said,
　　　　　　　　　　　　　went
away, would come back, first afflicted
　　　　　　　　　　　　　church,
what would be… We were caught in a

dream whispering names we'd forget
  waking up, caught waking up or in a
dream of waking up, moot sound riffling
    our lips. Nub was a name,   was

                              was

    a name,   a was a name, all moving
on... Names came after us, roused us in
  our sleep, the ballot-box opening grinned
and grinned again, gone we'd have been

                                    could

    we have run... It wasn't we were stuck,
    stood frozen, transfixed, Paralytic Dream #12...
It was waking known otherwise put running
  out of reach, nonsonance's waterless waves held
  us up, more than we could sense but

                              sensed

  even so, nonsonance's
gaptooth
slur

•

    Day late so all the old attunements gave
way, late but soon come even so... A
  political trek we'd have said it was
albeit politics kept us at bay,   nothing
                                wasn't
  politics we'd say. Wanting our want to
  be called otherwise, kept at bay though
  we were, day late but all the old stories
                             echoed

yet again, old but even so soon come... A
  mystic march they'd have said it was,
  acknowledging politics kept us at
bay,   everything was mystical
they'd say. Wanting our want to be
                    so
  named, kept at bay as we were,
                      what
  the matter was wasn't a question, no
                       ques-
tion what
it was

———————————

Nub no longer stood but lay and we
lay with it, earth-sway cradling our
backs. What the matter was rocked
us, a way we had with dirt, awaiting
                                    what
     already might have been there… Dust…
Abducted future… Dearth Lake's dry
     largesse… Dread Lakes' aliases, alibis,
                                        Death
     Lake also there… Where we were rubbed
          earth in our faces, a feeling we had
     for debris. Nub, no longer standing,
     filled the air, an exact powder, fell
                                        as
     we ran thru it, earth-sway swaddling
                                        our
     feet